W9-AFW-382

the
Intervention
Book

N Webster Comm Public Library
301 N Main St. PO Box 825
North Webster, IN 46555

the Intervention Book

Stories and Solutions from
Addicts, Professionals, and Families

Kathy L.

Conari Press

First published in 2011 by
Conari Press, an imprint of
Red Wheel/Weiser, LLC
with offices at:
665 Third Street, Suite 400
San Francisco, CA 94107
www.redwheelweiser.com

Copyright © 2011 by Kathy L.
All rights reserved. No part of this publication may be
reproduced or transmitted in any form or by any means, elec-
tronic or mechanical, including photocopying, recording, or by
any information storage and retrieval system, without permission in writing from Red Wheel/Weiser, LLC. Reviewers may
quote brief passages.

ISBN: 978-1-57324-495-4

Library of Congress Cataloging-in-Publication Data
is available upon request.

Cover design by Adrian Morgan
Cover photograph © iStockphoto.com
Interior by Stan Info
Typeset in Minion Pro

Printed in Canada
TCP
10 9 8 7 6 5 4 3 2 1
The paper used in this publication meets the minimum
requirements of the American National Standard for Information Sciences—Permanence of Paper for Printed Library Mate-
rials Z39.48-1992 (R1997).

I dedicate this book to my husband, John, who has stood by me through thick and thin for so many years, has been my biggest supporter, and has loved me like no one else could.

Contents

Foreword

One early May morning this year, I sat watching a DVR playback of myself talking about addiction and the power of intervention on *The Dr. Oz Show* and then *The Today Show*. I said a simple prayer, a thank you. In that moment, something new clicked for me. There I was, a recovered alcoholic, crystal meth addict, former bulimic, smoker, and pill popper, slinging my intervention dogma to millions on national television. I was helping others, sharing my belief that an invitational intervention is a powerful solution. And I was urging others to bust the myths of inaction and get to work.

Think of your own DVR moment. Hit "Play," and skip across the darkest days and times of your life. Now think of others' struggles. A precious life caught in an undertow of conflict, consumed by addictions to food, drugs, and/or alcohol. What can you do to help?

When Kathy asked me to contribute to her new book, I was thrilled. Intervention stories?! Sign me up. An intervention is what saved my life from the scrap heap, and Kathy and I both share the language of gratitude in our work. We made it through. In each story shared in this beautiful book, you'll see how all different kinds of families intervened to interrupt a loved one's addiction and crisis.

1

Years ago, I felt like there was no way to break the cycle of self-destruction. I was so low, so tired, so depressed. I didn't believe it was possible I could stop and stay stopped. I was broken, and broke down. I spun bigger and more implausible lies to cover up what I was really doing with my time, my body, and my money. I was constantly afraid of being found out. My friends knew something was wrong, but they didn't know I was addicted big time. Even as my career had gotten sweeter, the rest of my life was a sour patch of despair, defeat, and relationships that were stretched too thin.

Though I tried my best to hide my addictions, I knew my friends and family knew something was wrong. Truth be told, they were afraid I would say no if they tried to help. They feared they might make things worse if they intervened. From that fear came inaction, and they did nothing for decades. It's not their fault I suffered in addiction—but they had bought into one of the biggest lies of all: that someone has to want to change to be helped, and that he needs to hit bottom.

Would I die of shame if I was ever caught or called out on my bad behaviors? No, but shame was a powerful motivator to stay in my addictions. Here's the crazy truth—the day my friends confronted me and told me they knew that I was struggling, they knew I was doing something crazy and sick and sad, they knew I was in deep debt from my reckless lifestyle, was the day I was finally able to accept their help. My friends started a conversation with people who weren't afraid of my denial, my lies, or my hiding. They loved me and demonstrated that love and wouldn't take no for an answer, and then, *I let them help me*. That was the summer of 2002, more than eight years ago, and I've been clean and sober since soon after.

In 2009, I wrote a controversial book called *How to Change Someone You Love*. It rubbed some folks the wrong way because it challenged the old adage that you can't change anyone except yourself, and it's pointless to even try. Maybe it's true that one's essential personality and his or her likes and dislikes are pretty fixed. But in the context of addiction and self-destructive behaviors, I know from my own experience that other people did help me change. Without them stepping between me and my make-believe narrative of what was going on in my life, I know that today my life would either be a horrific nightmare, ten times worse than the lowest I ever got, or I'd be dead.

There are millions of people changed today because of the power of intervention, and I love that Kathy has collected stories of challenge, hope, and action—stories from the intervention front lines! Intervention comes in all shapes and sizes—from doctors to judges, to loved ones and co-workers. No matter the source or direction of the intervention, externally applied pressure can change folks for the good.

Some people are uncomfortable with the term "intervention." They think it's self-righteous and crosses the line of respecting someone's privacy, and I might agree if we were talking about trying to change someone's political or religious views. The way I define it, though, an intervention is about interrupting self-destructive behaviors with love. We are reminding someone that we care, we pay attention, and we see them for what they really are. And we know they are bigger and better than their nonsense of addiction and will help hold them accountable to making change.

My second book, *Just 10 LBS*, is a large scale intervention helping thousands of Americans take control of their eating habits, their bodies, and their lives. Intervention works! Love is the best motivation of all. "I love you. We're worried. We need help, so we're having a family meeting—with or without you," is how the invitation to my interventions usually start.

My work today as a board-registered interventionist is a calling I believe in. Of the thousands I've helped, I've never seen a family intervention make things worse. Period.

I challenge you to read this book and open your heart to the information and the inspiration in the stories you'll read here. At the end of your rope is hope and help. And this book has good bunches of both.

Onward,

Brad Lamm
May, 2011

Acknowledgments

A number of years ago, when I was out there looking for the happiness in life that seemed to elude me, I read every type of self-help book imaginable. I had been a student of yoga as exercise for a long time but was now wanting to feel it from the heart and soul. I worked hard at meditation, studied the chakras, tried to understand numerology, journaled, and read angel cards, totem cards, and anything else that I thought would open up something in my body, mind, and spirit.

Nothing worked because I was in the throes of a disease—alcoholism. I can't say that I was in denial during this time, because the idea of my being an alcoholic had not resonated with me one single bit. The denial came later when the doubts had crept in, but by then I had given up all the aforementioned activities.

The importance of this today is that when I was in my self-help mode, I visited a man known for chakra readings. It didn't come cheap, but I thought that perhaps he might give me a clue about my "misery and discontent," as I define that period today. He had never seen me before, or I him. As he looked at and read the colors in each of my chakra points, I was amazed at what he could see. When he got to the throat chakra, he asked me if I was a writer. My response was "No, but a lifelong ambition of mine is to write a book." "Well," he replied, "You will. It won't be a novel, but it will be a book of joy and hope." I asked him what I would be writing about, but he had absolutely no idea! Through the following years, while my life was spiraling downhill, I never forgot his words; I just figured he was wrong.

Three and a half years ago, I began writing for BellaOnline, an "e-zine" covering a ton of different topics. I became the 12-Step Recovery editor and have faithfully written on this topic each and every week. When I first began writing, I remembered what that chakra reader had told me and decided that maybe he was half right. I was writing for the public, but it wasn't the book he had told me about.

This past spring, I was approached by Conari Press about writing a book on interventions. This was *it!* This was what I had waited for since I was a little girl. I am in awe that I was chosen to write this book, but even more in awe because it was God's plan. Whenever I thought of writing, I could never come up with a subject I knew enough about or a topic I thought would be of interest. So it took years of drinking, literally killing myself each day, losing the "me" I knew, and almost losing everyone I loved in order to reach the point of a dream fulfilled. Of course, I would have preferred to write a book without all of the drama, but I can only say that God works in mysterious ways. Honestly, I truly feel that I have walked through hell and come out on the other side, not unscathed, but in the long run, a better person in most every way. Today, in recovery, I try to live the life my Creator intended for me to live. I have received countless gifts in sobriety, but one of the most important to me is being able to understand the nature of gratitude and, in doing so, live in gratitude.

I couldn't have written this book of joy, hope, and solutions without the help of so many people who were willing to take the time and effort to share with me because they believed in me and the message I wanted to share. As a teacher in another life, I believe the best way to learn something well is to teach it. The same is true for writing. If you want to know all you can about a subject, write about it. This is the hardest "job" I have ever had, but the result is that I know more not only about addiction and recovery, but also about myself. This is what this book is all about: hearing (or reading) what you are supposed to hear and taking action.

So let me first thank my Higher Power for life as I know it today and for being able to express my appreciation and thanks to the following:

To Karen Zazzera, Scottsdale Intervention; Jeff Schultz, Sonoran Healing Center; Scott Peterson; Holly Williamson, NCADD; Jan Scouten; Rick Benson, Algamus Recovery Centers; and Albert Gaulden, the Sedona Intensive, not only for their willingness to give me time and information but also for their passion and dedication to helping others. Thank you for your inspiration and for being true professionals.

To Deb Stelzleni, who helped change my life in positive ways and saw all the good in me when I wasn't able to or didn't want to myself; to Lisa Shea, editor of BellaOnline, for giving me the opportunity to write weekly on addiction and recovery for an international readership; to Amber Guetebier, Conari Press, for encouraging me and trusting that I had what it takes to successfully write this book and appreciating, but never feeding into, my addict behavior! To Barbara Joy, a fellow author, who has been my guide through this process and convinced me more than ever that there is no such thing as a coincidence.

The men and women who contributed their stories to this book will always hold a special place in my heart. To all of you, I applaud your honesty and willingness to share with me the details of your lives as addicts and subsequent recovery. I know that this is a painful process and that each of you shared your story out of fellowship and love for those who are addicted and for their families and friends. Thank you, my friends.

Throughout my years in recovery, I have met countless men and women who have in some way been instrumental to my ability to be able to write this today. To Maureen, Dara, Cynthia, Sue, the women I see at meetings each week, the women I have had the privilege of meeting and working with at Weldon House, the many email friends I have made throughout the world via BellaOnline, thank you all. Each one of you has something to do with the happiness I feel today, and I know that no matter where I go, if I needed your hand, it would be extended to me.

Thanks to my dear friend Suelynn and her mom, Alta Thompson, who read this manuscript and helped me edit when I couldn't bear to read it any longer! To my spiritual friend Paulette Bodeman who will always be a kindred spirit.

To my family: Mom, Dad, Patti, Gary, Tom, Lori, Dan, Scott, all your spouses, and your kids. I am not sure how to even thank all of you and God for being such an incredible family. Your love throughout the years, the support all of you have shown me, and your sincere willingness to help me with this book are truly a gift I can't even comprehend. It's a good thing these don't require any real payback except for my love because it would truly be impossible!

Last...to my daughters, Maryn and Amanda; their spouses, Jason and Joe; my real gifts of sobriety, my

The Intervention Book

grandbabies, Amelia, Egan, Talula, Salah, Rune, Severin, and Belgium. I can't imagine life without any of you. Your support from the beginning of my journey has made me strong and has made life so worthwhile. Thank you for always being there for me and for those precious babies that I can so enjoy in sobriety.

To my dearest husband, John, I already dedicated this book to you. Need I say more?

May God bless all of you and keep you.

Introduction

Nobody can go back and start a new beginning but anyone can start today and make a new ending.
—Maria Robinson

THERE ARE FEW PEOPLE IN the country today who have not heard the word "intervention." It is a topic that is no longer confined to discussion behind closed doors but available to all on any one of a variety of TV programs.

Those of us in any type of recovery who watch these reality shows understand the addictions and behaviors; we cringe at the enablers and silently pray that the addict will agree to get help. If the help is accepted, we then begin guessing if the person will stay in recovery or not and what will happen based on that decision. We root in our living rooms for the ones who stay sober and wonder why they just didn't get it when they don't. In watching these programs, it is important to not only look at the behavior of the addict, but also

Every addiction is a family disease.

11

at how it affects family and friends. Every addiction is a family disease.

It would be great if every addict in the world got the opportunity offered those we see on TV. The reality is that

The road is different for every person.

very few addicts come face to face with a living, breathing interventionist. Nevertheless, addicts *do* recover and can stay sober for the rest of their lives. Recovery for any addict is not about willpower, but a series of bottoms, one or one hundred interventions, perhaps a "moment of clarity" (a self-realization that the addict wants to stop), and both a willingness and a desire to get well.

The journey from addiction to recovery can take an incredible amount of time, and the road is different for every person. During this stage, people, situations, and experiences can become the interventionist or the intervention. Each time the addict encounters an opportunity to break free in any form, there is that much more of a chance that he will begin to see the light. With these encounters, it may not be obvious to anyone on the outside that there is one iota of awareness in the addict. Little by little, though, they chip away at him physically, emotionally, and psychologically.

One of the common threads that I found in interviewing addicts for this book is that unless someone wants to recover, it will not happen. People who have formal interventions with a trained professional still may not be willing at all. Some will find that willingness once they are removed from their environment; others will not. It doesn't mean they will never get into recovery; it only means not right now.

I do not believe anyone recovers from an addiction without an intervention of some kind. Based on my own recovery and what I have discovered from others, there are three types of interventions: formal, informal, and divine. We'll look at each one of these to define them, discuss them briefly, and share an example. These categories are not based on scientific research. They are based on the common threads to be found in the stories of the recovered and on the fact that I know and can be 100 percent sure that no one can break out of an addiction alone. Something as simple as a self-help book—which God knows we have all devoured in our disease—or as devastating as a suicide attempt can be an intervention in and of itself.

You will notice that each chapter and each story begin with a quotation. I chose these particular words because either I felt they had relevance here, or, in some cases, I just love the quote. I invite you to find the meaning in each for yourself.

There is a chapter dedicated to what happens after an intervention or when the person decides to begin recovery. There is so much information about addiction counselors and rehab facilities that I could only give generalities. If you are beginning to understand addiction, whether it be for you or a loved one, I think the information will be helpful in planning and beginning the process. Of course, you can always pick up the phone book and call for help, but you should still understand how it all works to get an idea of how it can work for you. In a crisis, most of us don't think clearly, so hopefully this information will prompt you to begin your own education.

The majority of this book is a compilation of true stories told to me by addicts in recovery. I have had the unique opportunity of hearing each one directly from the source. I, in turn, have become something of a storyteller! As we are all unique beings, each story is unique to the addict who was willing to share. Not one of these had the same experiences, but the common thread is that someone or something in their lives brought each to a turning point. There was a moment of clarity that led to the beginning of a new way of life. Each person had one or more interventions of the various types, even if they had only one with a professional. Most addicts will credit their recovery to the last person or experience that brought them out of their disease. All will acknowledge, though, that God was instrumental in the entire process.

If you think you know the stereotypical addict, I have no doubt that the stories here will change your mind.

Each person who shared a story did so in order to inspire another addict or someone who loves and/or cares for an addict. The stories come from alcoholics, drug addicts, sex addicts, love addicts, gambling addicts, those with food disorders, and their families. Many of these folks are dual or poly-addicted.

If you think you know the stereotypical addict, I have no doubt that the stories here will change your mind. These "shares" are the real-life experiences (trust me, I couldn't make some of this stuff up) of both men and women ranging from age twenty to sixty-something. They are single, married, divorced; they are high school grads and holders of master's degrees; they are low-income and wealthy; they have kids or grandkids or no kids; and they come from all corners of the world. They are so different from one another you could probably find more similarities by rounding up a random group of people at an airport! This is the nature of addiction: equal opportunity for all!

As you read each story, I invite you to witness their early years, the beginnings of their addiction, and their bottoms, and recognize the interventions that take place. Some will seem huge and some quite small. Look at the behaviors of the family and friends that may have *This is the nature of addiction: equal opportunity for all!* enabled the addict. You will read experiences that will seem unfathomable (and are even to me), and you won't be able to believe that the addict just keeps plugging along in disease. The nature of addiction can be so powerful it can outdo human nature at its worst: ranging from abandoning your children, prostitution, prison, being committed to an asylum, DUIs, and suicide attempts to rape, theft, and more as experienced by mothers, fathers, brothers, sisters, friends, and neighbors. These are real people! I have not added one single enhancement to any one of these stories. I didn't have to. My personal 12-Step recovery program suggests that I look for similarities and not differences. The behaviors of the addict are remarkably the same, although experiences vary considerably. The addict has to undergo a psychic change so that a meaningful recovery can begin. You will see that as well.

This book is for anyone and everyone. If you are an addict, if you think you are an addict, or if you have a friend or loved one in any type of addiction, I offer you hope and solutions. The message of my friends who share in this book is that they have found a life today outside of addiction. Some of these people have truly stood on the brink of hell and are grateful to their Higher Power and all those interventions and interventionists who chipped away at their armor. Their willingness to share with me and you is their way of offering a measure of faith and hope that anything is possible.

Each of these stories has a beginning and a middle, but unlike stories you have read elsewhere, they have no end. As the storyteller, I can only tell you where each story stops at "today." The ending is still to be revealed and can only be found one day at a time. Intervention is the beginning of a process; recovery is a lifetime commitment.

Namaste. May you walk your journey in peace and harmony.

Chapter I

To Family and Friends Who Want to Intervene

The best thing you can give yourselves... is the gift of possibility. And the best thing you can give each other is the pledge to go on protecting that gift in each other as long as you live.

—Paul Newman

I KNOW HOW DIFFICULT IT is to watch a loved one spiral downward because of an addiction. Actually, since I was the addicted one, I know that however much I might have believed I was the victim, the real victims were my family and friends who cared. If it were not for their love and support, I would not have been able to begin recovery and maintain my sobriety.

Intervention does not have to wait until the addict is facing illness and/or death. It does not have to be put off until she is facing homelessness or the legal system. Intervention can begin long before an addict reaches a bottom.

No one knows when or what that bottom will be, because there are no predictors and it is different for everyone. In other words, what are you waiting for?

There are many ways you can intervene, but none are easy. If the addict could be reached through normal conversation, there would be no reason for me to be writing this today. If it were easy, professional interventionists and most of the rehab facilities out there wouldn't need to exist. It requires time and patience, support, education, and, most of all, taking care of you and your family first.

Intervention does not have to wait until the addict is facing illness and/or death.

I have been told that where there is an addict, you'll have one or more enablers and codependents. This is what makes addiction affect an entire group of people, most often a family. There is an amazing trickle-down effect within the family, and so even if a person thinks he is the only one affected, he is wrong.

This is a real-life example of what happens within the family starting with one addict and one enabler. I have a friend who is a single mom with four adult children. The youngest is an alcoholic. My friend knows this. Everyone knows this. No one is in denial except for the alcoholic himself. She also knows she should not be doing the things she is doing to support him, but as a mom, she just doesn't know where to draw the line. The enabling doesn't stop with her, though. It has spread into the larger family unit through her. The extended family includes her other children and their spouses, her parents, and all her brothers and sisters and their spouses. Because my friend is loving and kind and would give away her last cent, the entire family wants to help her. Unfortunately, the kind of help she asks for always revolves around her addict son. For example, she may need to borrow a car because her son needs transportation to work. He totaled his vehicle, and so in order for him to make some type of a living, he needs to get to his job. So family members offer to help her by giving her their cars. They all mean well, but they enable her to enable him. This is the spiral that destroys families slowly but surely.

She needs to get help, if not for him, then for herself. An analogy that makes sense is with the safety instructions you get before flying. Before taking off, the flight attendant goes through the whole safety routine. One of the demonstrations is for the oxygen mask. The attendant clearly tells travelers how to put on the mask in the case of a sudden drop in cabin pressure, but the most important thing conveyed to passengers is that if they are traveling with children, they must put on their own mask first and *then* help the child.

I could not think of a better example illustrating how the parent, spouse, or other family members of an addict must get help first before helping their loved one; even if the loved one doesn't want an "oxygen mask."

Family members or friends who are concerned with the addiction(s) of a loved one can take care of themselves first and foremost by attending 12-Step meetings. They are available and free! It is the first step toward understanding. It is the first step in taking control of your own life and not permitting it to be ruled by an addiction. Everyone hears his own story in these rooms (similarities, not differences), and the support a family receives gives them the strength and the impetus to move forward. Twelve-Step meetings for the family may be the launching pad for seeking counseling for themselves and for their addicted family member. Many family members go into residential treatment programs, as many facilities have designed therapy programs specifically for families.

I have made sure to include a few stories shared by those not addicted. The stories of "Kelly," "Tracy," "Jody," "Lori," and "Katherine" are of family members and loved ones who have lived through addiction and recovery and offer their advice on what worked for them.

If you have intervened in your addict's life and both of you are working a recovery program, congratulations! You can be assured that there is a place in heaven for you! If you have an addict in your life and are not sure what steps to take, I hope that you will find some of the answers here. You can be instrumental in the intervention if you are willing to understand the addict's disease and listen to those who will support you. Your choice may be to consult a professional for a formal intervention. It may also be your choice to intervene in smaller, less formal ways. It is up to you; there is no totally correct solution for everyone. The important thing is that you find help in some way.

Regardless of how you pursue intervention, I hope and pray that you will find freedom for yourself and for the addict in your life.

Chapter II

Formal Intervention

The real gift of intervention is that I want to relieve the family of the burden of thinking that they have to take care of the person for the rest of their lives. They really need to let go of that in a loving way, not a walled-off way, and give the person the dignity and respect to be their own individual and take care of themselves. If everyone does that, the cream rises to the top.

—Karen Zazzera, MC, LPC, BRI-II addiction counselor and interventionist

THE WORD "FORMAL" IS NOT one you will see often to describe an intervention. I didn't make it up, but it is not a common term in intervention literature. For the purposes of this book, I'm using "formal intervention" to refer to a specific type of intervention that involves sitting down with the addict to confront the situation. It's best done with the help of a professional interventionist.

You might think that due to the exposure addictions now have on the Internet, on reality TV, and through the sensationalism that surrounds the fall of certain celebrities, more families and friends would pursue help for their addicted loved ones. The truth is more than 23 million Americans are believed to have an addiction, yet only 10 percent of those receive treatment. Many of the people not in treatment choose instead to dive headfirst into a 12-Step recovery program, just as I did.

More than 23 million Americans are believed to have an addiction, yet only 10 percent of those receive treatment.

So you have watched TV, and you think it looks easy enough to get the family together and try this intervention thing on your own. Professionals would advise against that, as there are many components of an intervention, and you don't want to compromise what is a great opportunity to help. In this chapter, I hope to give you a better understanding of what a formal intervention is so that you can make an informed decision about whether this option is right for your situation.

There are many counselors and therapists working in the field of addiction. There are psychiatrists, and there are psychologists. Some interventionists focus on addressing a particular type of addiction, while others are open to assist with any problems involving addiction. So, how can you find an advisor who's right for your needs?

The Association of Intervention Specialists (AIS) website (*associationofinterventionspecialists.org*) is a good place to start. The AIS is a network of interventionists located throughout the country and abroad. All full members are Board Registered Interventionists, and they have met or exceeded the association's educational and performance standards. All members adhere to the AIS Code of Ethics. There are two levels of membership: full members and candidates. All members will be either a BRI-I or a BRI-II. A BRI-I title means that the interventionist holds credentials to work in the area of drugs and alcohol only and have been doing interventions for a minimum of two years. A BRI-II title means that the counselor is certified to hold interventions for more than alcohol and drugs (sex, gambling, eating disorders, and mental illness, for example) and has been doing interventions for at least five years.

At the time this book is being written, registration for interventionists is voluntary. Many universities and private companies offer their own certification programs, too. When researching a potential interventionist to assist you, check out the candidate's qualifications, experience, and success rate.

Because there aren't yet standardized certification requirements to be an interventionist, theoretically, anyone could take on the role of interventionist. In some cases, recovered addicts become counselors to help others with their recovery. Fairly new to sobriety themselves, these counselors could think their own recovery experience is all it takes to assist with staging interventions. But in fact, staging a successful intervention is a nuanced process, and it takes experience and education to plan it appropriately. And although addictions have many similarities, the approach to intervention isn't always the same. Compulsive gamblers, for example, generally have strong egos, so such a person might be approached with a different energy than the more fragile food addict would be. This does not mean that there are no qualified counselors out there doing interventions; it only means that before choosing an interventionist, you should have a good idea of their background and formal education.

We talk about bottoms quite a bit in recovery. I have to say that I don't know one addicted person, regardless of the addiction, who did not hit a bottom, some more than once. But a family doesn't have to wait for a bottom, until the addict has lost everything, to intervene. Putting off an intervention keeps the addict in her disease and the family in their disease also. Even if the intervention felt like a failure because the addict denied there was a problem, it most likely was not. It goes back to what I said earlier about putting a chink in the armor. Some addicts need quite a few of these before they consider recovery.

Recently, I had the opportunity to interview Karen Zazzera, MC, LPC, BRI-II, of Scottsdale Intervention. Based on research I've gathered on interventions and the role of professional interventionists, I would say Karen's experience typifies how most interventionists work with clients. The intervention process begins with a phone call to the interventionist. Any concerned person could make the first call, but Karen told me the initial contact usually comes from a woman, perhaps the mother or wife of an addict. A first meeting is arranged so that the interventionist can do a full assessment and so the client can interview the interventionist. The trust and comfort level a client has for the interventionist is extremely important. If the client decides to proceed with an intervention, there will be two more preparatory sessions of about three hours. The sessions before the intervention usually involve the intervention team either in person or by Skype or conference call, family members, and perhaps close friends of the addict who is to be the beneficiary. There is discussion about not only the beneficiary but also how each family member or friend might be playing into the addiction (enabling). The family and interventionist also decide whether certain family members or friends should be present. The type of intervention is discussed as well as the strategy. The family and friends write letters to the addicted person, which will be read at the intervention. There is discussion about which treatment facility will be chosen and who will take the beneficiary to that center. Then a treatment plan might be established for the family members. The intervention comes next and could last from one to three hours.

The type of intervention depends on what the client is looking for, but in Karen's practice, she offers the "surprise" intervention (clinically called the "Johnson Model") and the "invitational" intervention. Depending on the particular addiction, she may recommend one or the other, but it usually is the family who chooses. Most families initially opt for the surprise because they believe if the addicts know what's going on, they won't show up. The truth is that they do come at least 89 percent of the time. The invitational intervention takes longer, and so it is harder on the family because during the family meetings, everyone—not just the beneficiary—is making commitments for a healthy change. Sometimes the beneficiary doesn't show up for the first scheduled family meeting, in which case another meeting, is scheduled, then another, until everyone can sit down together. The family system is imposed upon in an invitational. Often family members or friends may be flying in from other areas to participate, and doing this more than once is a hardship. It requires that the family change more for the invitational than the surprise intervention.

The weakness of a surprise intervention is that less is required of family members, and their own refusal to change can make the intervention ineffective. There is still a great deal of effort focused on the family for making commitments to change during the surprise intervention, but it is not as thorough as the invitational. There are times when the surprise changes to an invitational because the addict is told or finds out. It then becomes more of a family meeting to which he is invited to come. Regardless of the type of intervention, Karen's requirement of families is to "show up, speak your truth, offer help in a dignified and respectful way, stop enabling, go to family week when the beneficiary does enter treatment, and go to 12-Step meetings."

Show up, speak your truth, offer help in a dignified and respectful way.

Any type of intervention is draining. Most families are very emotional throughout the process, and the interventionist asks a lot of them. The family must make commitments and changes and be prepared to back them up. The family is as instrumental to the intervention as the addict is. Family members and friends must be totally on board and supportive. Most of the time, people want to do the right thing, and so once they understand that what they are doing is killing the person they love, they become willing to change. The interventionist finds out during the pre-intervention meetings if everyone asked to be present can actually be part of the process.

The interventionist is a moderator and a guide. The family members are the ones who really do the intervention and know the addicted person well and how to approach the issue. The family does most of the talking and is the true power behind the intervention.

When I ask Karen what happens if the addict refuses treatment, the good news she shares is that it doesn't happen often, but when it does, the family has already written the letter outlining the changes they are going to make to stop enabling the addiction. And that is a huge step on their part. An intervention never means someone is forced to go to treatment, because it is the right of each person to choose. I love the phrase Karen uses: "Addiction is not a choice, but recovery is." Each person in the family can go about their own lives knowing that they have done everything they possibly can. They can let go of guilt and complete responsibility for the addicted person. They will have learned through the process how each person must care for himself. This helps the family to break free from the addiction. They can still love the addict, but they do not have to love or honor the disease.

Addiction is not a choice, but recovery is.

The best-case scenario is that the intervention ends and the subject accepts the help offered. What next? First of all, everyone must recognize that the intervention is only the first step and the road ahead requires patience and action.

Whether the addict is going away for treatment or staying close to home, she may go through detox. Withdrawal can be life threatening. Every good treatment center knows the protocol. They know the correct "cocktail" of drugs to detox the person; they monitor and medically supervise. Detox usually takes the first three to five days of treatment. The amount of time is usually a best guess because family members often do not have any idea how much the person drank or drugged, and addicts tend to downplay the amount of alcohol or drugs they used. Not all drug addicts need detox, but most alcoholics do. Although some do not show serious signs of withdrawal, a treatment center may not want to take that chance. Withdrawal symptoms tend to emerge after the third day of withdrawal and vary from person to person.

It is pretty standard for addicts to move on to a residential treatment center after an intervention. The reason for this is that by the time of an intervention, according to Karen, the addiction is severe. They are in quite a bit of denial, or they wouldn't even need an intervention. Where they go for treatment depends on a number of things. Young people (ages fourteen to twenty-five) might be best off a distance from the home because the level of peer pressure can be too great. If you have a professional person who wants to hang on to a career, that addict may stay local where it is easier to have family contact, even if that can also be a "mixed bag."

The most important consideration about where a person goes to treatment is that it be the most clinically appropriate treatment match for him and offer the resources he needs. Location is really secondary. There are residential treatment centers that accept patients with any addiction. There are some, for example, that will accept alcoholics and drug addicts but have more of a focus on sex addictions. There are others that are addiction-specific, such as for gambling. If you have found the right interventionist for your family, then that counselor can guide you to the proper facility based on the addiction, the severity of the addiction, geography, the length of treatment, and the financial resources of the family. It is also important that the interventionist has physically been to the facility, has talked to the staff, and walked the property.

Another option that may be recommended is intensive outpatient (IOP) care. This means that the addict/patient sleeps at home. IOP programs can also bolster recovery when the person leaves a long-term residential facility.

These are usually a six- to eight-week program of two to three days per week for about three hours each. The patient may then continue working with a therapist. According to Karen, studies show that people are most successful in recovery if they stay in treatment longer. Ninety days is usually a good choice, but not everyone gets that opportunity, because of finances or other considerations.

Since addiction is a family disease, a treatment plan for everyone in the family might be suggested. Family members will need to change, too, and there are many workshops, short residential programs, and 12-Step recovery programs available to families.

The addict has now gone through the intervention, detox, and has completed the prescribed rehab. Now what? There is no cure for addiction, and so it is important for the addict to continue seeing the interventionist. There is deep work to be done, and it takes time and patience. The interventionist becomes the counselor, and now it is about helping the addict with many issues. Staying clean isn't enough for long-term sobriety. Twelve-Step programs are the lifeline for addicts all over the world and are recommended by most interventionists and counselors.

There is deep work to be done, and it takes time and patience.

So it should be clear now that a formal intervention and the ensuing rehab involve many steps, and you should have a picture of how a professional interventionist can help you and your loved one through them. If you are still considering "going it alone," and let's face it, some families do choose this, here are a few thoughts. Anyone can offer an addicted person help. Family members can ask someone they love to go to treatment, they can offer to take them, and they can pay for it. At that point, that is all they can do. There are numerous organizations and 12-Step programs that can assist through their literature or on the phone to help the family become educated in terms of understanding the addict. However, many times when families attempt to intervene alone, sessions can deteriorate into angry outbursts, defensiveness, begging, and pleading. None of this is motivating for anyone involved. There is a reason why there are professionals in the area of intervention. There is an art to bringing a family together to help someone they love. The offer of treatment must be presented in a manner the person can hear and accept. It's not easy.

Step past any fear you might have and take the first step to save the addict in your life, yourself, and your entire family.

Do interventions work? All treatment centers monitor their outcomes, and you can get all types of statistics when you ask for them. You might hear 60 percent; you might hear 99 percent. Of all people who go into treatment, there are three groups: self-referred, court-referred, and intervention-referred. Karen offers an interesting statistic: More people stayed clean after being intervention-referred than from the other two groups. Why? It is all about the family getting on board and the support system. (Incidentally, the court-referred is second, followed by self-referral.) Not everyone who has an intervention goes directly into recovery. There are some who will hold out a few days, a few weeks, or even a month after an intervention. They end up going because the family sticks to their commitments and their bottom lines and no longer enables the addict.

Addiction is a disease. Don't make excuses for your sons and daughters when they drink or take drugs, thinking that this is a phase that they will grow out of. When you read the stories I tell later on in this book, you will realize that none of these people outgrew their addiction when they became adults. Is that something you are willing to risk? Alcohol is not the leading culprit for young people today. It's all about drugs. Marijuana is a gateway drug. It leads to other drugs, and for kids under twenty-one, drugs are a lot easier to get then alcohol. Kids today are not even starting on wine and beer but on prescription drugs because mom, dad, grandma, and grandpa have plenty in the medicine cabinet. Kids are going to "pharm parties" and have no clue what kind of medications they are even ingesting.

Age makes no difference. No one is too young or too old to have a formal intervention. Karen tells me her oldest patient was eighty-eight. Someone loved him enough to give him the gift of recovery even at that age.

There is a tremendous amount of hope for any of you who want a loved one to get healthy and sober. Words of love and care to an addict or asking for a promise from an addict will get you nowhere. Stop enabling. A formal intervention starts with the family. Step past any fear you might have and take the first step to save the addict in your life, yourself, and your entire family. Life is good. Really!

Shawna

How privileged we are to understand so well the divine paradox that strength rises from weakness; that humiliation goes before resurrection; that pain is not only the price but the very touchstone of spiritual rebirth.

—Bill W.

When I met Shawna, she was about eight months pregnant with baby number three. She had a two- and a four-year-old and was working full-time, so I was very happy that she could give me a bit of her time. Her story may not be as detailed or as long as some of the others, but that doesn't change the message that hope springs eternal!

Shawna is thirty-three years old, married, and now the mother of three. She delivered not long after we spoke. She is an alcoholic in recovery for eight and a half years now. Do the math, and you can see that she recovered at a very early age.

Shawna's maternal grandfather was an alcoholic, and she suffered a mentally-ill mother and an absentee father. Shawna took her first drink at twelve because she was home alone and knew she wasn't supposed to touch it. She was seventeen when she began to drink alcoholically, and during the eight long years of her active addiction, she remembers stopping one time for a period of about a week.

Few teenagers/young adults see themselves as alcoholics, since they don't fit that stereotype of the bum with the bottle in a paper bag.

There was no *real* denial at that time about being an alcoholic, because she never thought about it. Few teenagers/young adults see themselves as alcoholics, since they don't fit that stereotype of the bum with the bottle in a paper bag. Shawna says she didn't want to stop. She loved alcohol and drinking.

Today Shawna admits that she was a binge drinker and put herself in numerous dangerous situations. She dabbled in drugs, and the combination of the drugs and alcohol gave her a heart attack. She passed out everywhere:

cars, bars, bathrooms, the backseats of taxicabs, and she was usually by herself. If there were family engagements, Shawna never attended. She would make plans with the people she really cared about, especially her younger brothers, but didn't follow through. The hardest thing for Shawna was being in her disease when her paternal grandfather died. He had helped raise her, and she loved him very much. She loved the drinking more.

Shawna is a college graduate and worked a full-time job but drank socially every night after work. Unlike many alcoholics who increase their alcohol intake over a period of time, Shawna says she doesn't really remember drinking in the morning and is sure she never went to work drunk—hung over and tired, maybe, but never drunk.

She sought out people who wanted to spend their evenings like she did, and that was drinking, smoking, and playing bar games. On weekends she would go to a club so she could dance and drink. If she had to attend a function that did not involve alcohol, she was extremely uncomfortable.

As her drinking got worse and worse, Shawna's friends began to notice that maybe she drank a bit more than she should. When they mentioned it to her, she felt ashamed, humiliated, and also embarrassed. While early in her drinking career Shawna was not aware enough to be in denial, she was now. She honestly didn't think she was an alcoholic. She says, "I didn't have any idea what alcoholism looked like."

Everyone has a bottom, and Shawna was no different. One evening when she was out with friends, she passed out in the bathroom of a bar—as she had done many times before. This time her friends took her out to sleep in their car, but when they drove her home three hours later, she wouldn't wake up. She was living at her mom's house at the time, and her little brother woke up. He got her mom, and they drove Shawna to the hospital. She came to on the way there. The first thing the doctor did was draw blood. After four to five hours of not drinking, Shawna's blood alcohol level came back as a .25! The doctor told her mom very clearly that Shawna had an alcohol problem. Her mom (by now divorced from her dad) was dating a DUI attorney. He was able to direct her to a treatment center and find the people who would be involved in an intervention.

Unbeknownst to Shawna, her mother consulted with a treatment counselor who suggested she do a "soft" intervention. This intervention was led by her mom. Her grandmother had also called some of Shawna's friends, but after finding out about this, Shawna laughed and said she "didn't think the drinking buddies were comfortable with that."

During the intervention, Shawna was confronted about her drinking and with the medical evidence from her recent trip to the ER. Her mother also told her that she was no longer permitted to come home if she had been drinking. Shawna says her first emotional response was anger; then she felt terrified. She could *not* imagine not drinking. The thought made her go into a full-blown panic.

Shawna says her first emotional response was anger; then she felt terrified.

After the intervention, Shawna wanted to prove she was not an alcoholic. She began to research alcoholism, thinking for sure she would find proof that she didn't have it, but couldn't find anything to back her up. She then tried to just control her drinking, like maybe one drink per hour.

Shawna became more convinced that she was an alcoholic and so went into an intensive outpatient (IOP) program. The IOP was three times per week for three hours for about two months. She completed the IOP and a follow-up program and then began to go to 12-Step meetings on her own.

Shawna has never relapsed in her eight and a half years, but she says she came close when she was on pain medication. She ended up throwing the meds away and calling a recovery friend to talk about it.

Even though it was her mother who called the counselor and initiated the intervention, Shawna's family wasn't particularly supportive of her sobriety. She still lived with her mom, but there was alcohol in the house. The friends she made in outpatient treatment and the recovery fellowship became her foundation. Shawna firmly believes that "God guided me to the women friends I have in the program."

Today she maintains her sobriety through prayer and a spiritual connection to her Higher Power. She believes this connection happens through attending meetings and reaching out to friends in recovery. She surrounds herself with people who live the same lifestyle—no alcohol—including her spouse, who has never had a drink due to religious beliefs.

I ask Shawna what advice she would give someone who shares her addiction to alcohol. Her advice would be "get to a meeting," and she would even offer to take them. She enjoys sharing her experience, strength, and hope because she believes that this outreach is a significant part of a 12-Step program. This is that special connection and understanding addicts have with one another.

If you have an addict in your life, Shawna believes that it is helpful to do research and read. Attend a 12-Step meeting for family members, and do it right away! This is where you will get support. Contact treatment centers as well as an intervention specialist to try to help your loved one hear the message. She also says that it is important for addicts to know that the disease is not their fault and not in their control. "I don't believe there is anything another person can do to keep someone sober. It's a choice the alcoholic has to make for himself or herself, but family and friends can carry the message."

Shawna's life today is one of peace, happiness, and, most of all, acceptance.

Chapter III

Informal Interventions

People spend a lifetime searching for happiness, looking for peace. They chase idle dreams, addictions, religions, even other people, hoping to fill the emptiness that plagues them. The irony is the only place they ever needed to search was within.

—Ramona L. Anderson

THE COUNTERPART OF THE FORMAL intervention is the "informal" kind. When I agreed to write a book on intervention, I thought I would find an equal amount of formal to informal interventions. I was so wrong. The more I researched and talked to people in recovery, the more I realized that the majority of addicts recover without a formal intervention. I had taken an unscientific poll in a few different groups of recovering addicts, and out of these groups of about twenty-plus each, only one person had actually had a formal intervention.

This is not to say that certified, professional interventionists do not play a major role in assisting and guiding families into helping their loved ones get sober. These people as well as other qualified addiction specialists, therapists, and counselors still work with the addict after a decision has been made to get sober. Professional, certified interventionists are seldom approached until the family is desperate (as indicated in chapter II). Recovery is a process, as is the onset of an addiction to the point of admitting the addiction. No one aspires to become an addict. A quote from St. Augustine captures this perfectly: "Habit, if not resisted, soon becomes necessity." That is not to say that all habits become addictions, but that first drink, drug, bet, purge, or chat room could be the beginning for some, especially if they are genetically predisposed. Drinking, drugging, gambling, eating, sex, shopping, smoking, and more begin as habits but become the center of an addict's life. They are more than necessities: They become "gods" that are worshipped each and every day.

So what exactly do I mean by an "informal" intervention? It encompasses any person or event that plants a seed of change in an addict's thinking. Each can be the beginning of bringing someone out of denial. Most addicts don't wake up one morning and say "Gee, I think I'll get into recovery today." I do not know of anyone, anywhere, who is addicted to anything and made that decision on her own and stayed clean. An informal intervention is a series of encounters with people and events that begin to give the addict pause as to where his life is going and what can be done.

Addicts in recovery will attribute their decision to get help to the last memorable person or event—the thing that made them hit bottom and, for the first time, look up. The truth is before that bottom, there were a series of people and events in any addict's life that actually took hold but were not recognized at the time. For example, many spouses take it hard if a total stranger is instrumental in getting their wife or husband clean. They are happy about the change, of course, but wonder why they weren't "the one" after so many years of pleading and begging. I don't believe any of the pleading and begging was ignored. I believe that on a subconscious level, those were informal interventions that brought the addict closer and closer to the moment they could accept help.

One of the counselors I talked to, Jan Scouten, LISAC, is a clinical supervisor for an outpatient treatment facility. He explained this to me, and I think it makes my "chink in the armor" theory more clear. He uses DUIs as an example. In this case, the court or legal system is the interventionist. If you have a certain number of people arrested for a DUI, about half of this group will never get another one because either they don't have an alcohol or drug problem or they found a way to stop any abuse. The other half goes on to the next level, and at that point there are successes (movements toward recovery), but there are still failures. The screening continues. It doesn't mean those who have failed are not paying the price. They are. They may only get the help they need in prison and may be clean at the end of their time or begin again. The point is that any one addict may have to go through a series of interventions, some with consequences as serious as going to jail for a DUI and some not so serious, before choosing recovery.

Even families who decide to have a formal intervention try the informal route first. As I noted in chapter II, the addict does not have to hit bottom before a formal intervention is sought, but it seems that most do. There are interventionists in the lives of every addict: the doctor who suggests that the addict has serious physical issues because of her addiction, the boss who fires the addict because he can't work a full week or even a full day, the police officer who stops the addict for a violation and serves a DUI, the judge who throws the addict into jail for twenty-four hours or more, the CPS worker who threatens to take the addict's children, the CPS worker who does take the children, the spouse or parent of an addict who goes to a 12-Step recovery group to find help for the addict only to realize she is equally addicted, the divorce papers that arrive in the mail, the arrest for shoplifting, and so many more. As many addicts as there are out there, probably an equal number of informal interventions.

It takes only one person or event to finally tilt the scale in the direction of recovery.

Even though these may not be enough for an addict to overcome denial, each is one more thing in the arsenal that will bring the person closer to a decision to recover. There are those who never recover from an addiction, just as there are those who never recover from a physical or mental disease. But as long as there is faith in a Higher Power and a willingness to help, anything is possible. There are many lives lost due to addiction, but your loved one or you do not have to be one of these.

It takes only one person or event to finally tilt the scale in the direction of recovery. There may have been years of people and events that would seem to be enough for the addict to change, but he doesn't until it is time. Most of the addicts who share their stories in this book had countless informal interventions, but there was one last person or event—"the straw that broke the camel's back"—that set recovery into motion.

Everyone can be an everyday interventionist. When we share in 12-Step meetings, we talk about hearing what we are supposed to hear. Never underestimate that. You may have said something to your addicted loved one 100 times, but maybe the 101st will be when you get through. One of the resounding themes in the stories is that the addict has to want to recover. Patience is a requirement if you are trying to be of help. Please remember that, no matter what the situation, you do not have to wait for the addict to recover before finding help for yourself and your family. If you choose not to get involved with a formal intervention, your informal one can be taking care of yourself and the rest of your family.

Everyone can be an everyday interventionist.

When you read the stories here, don't judge anyone, but look closely at the characters who are involved with the addict: the parents, friends, siblings, coworkers, and others. How do these people help the addict toward recovery? How do they enable the addict? These are real stories, and if you are reading this book, you are probably an addict or have one in your life. Your story is just as real. I hope that you will find something in any one of them that will be what you need to read and hear.

Mary G.

Overcome any bitterness that may have come because you were not up to the magnitude of pain entrusted to you. Like the mother of the world who carries the pain of the world in her heart, you are sharing in a certain measure of that cosmic pain and are called upon to meet it in joy instead of self-pity.

—Pir Vilayat Khan

Not everyone is lucky enough to get sober early on in life. Truth be told, getting sober at any age is a gift from God. Mary is fifty-seven years old and has been in recovery for seven years. Her only regret today is wondering why it took so long for her to get to the wonderful life she has now. It was God's plan.

Most of the addicts that I have interviewed had alcoholic or drug-addicted parents. Mary is no different. She doesn't remember her earliest years, but by the time she was sixteen, she was well aware of the dysfunction in her family. Her mom drank nightly, and her dad enjoyed wine and marijuana. Dad left mom for someone a few years younger than Mary. She has two brothers. One built a winery and has begun to abuse alcohol and the other went to rehab about twenty-five years ago but has since started taking Vicodin, Percoset, and morphine due to a back injury.

Her first drink was also her first drunk. It didn't make any difference that she vomited profusely.

Mary's first drink was at the age of fifteen. Her parents were out of town, and someone brought alcohol to her house. Mary said her first drink was also her first drunk. It didn't make any difference that she vomited profusely. She loved the feeling of being drunk, because who doesn't want to feel prettier, funnier, and smarter?

After high school, a friend offered her speed and a cigarette. Mary loved the feeling. Cigarettes continued to be a thirty-nine-year habit, and if you are a smoker or an ex-smoker, you will understand how difficult this addiction is. Nicotine, as Mary told me, consumed her life, actions, and thoughts. She also added marijuana to the menu. All three became a daily routine: Speed to get going, nicotine throughout the day, and weed to settle down at night.

Mary's boyfriend since the seventh grade went into the Air Force, and about one week after he left, Mary gave up the idea of going to college and decided to give herself a year to party instead. She was introduced to a dealer. Nine months later, that dealer became her husband. She was nineteen years old. They were married for thirteen years (no children, thank God), and in that period of time he introduced her to mescaline, LSD, peyote, and cocaine.

Mary was also drinking every day. It began with Southern Comfort, but that was too sweet. She switched to tequila, but that was too expensive. Then she tried vodka and grapefruit juice, and that was just right! Healthy, in fact, was her joke. Making jokes about drinking helped to support the denial about drinking too much. Mary also began to find a different

Mary began to find a different liquor store to go to daily, so the clerks wouldn't think she was an alcoholic.

liquor store to go to daily, so the clerks wouldn't think she was an alcoholic. She honestly didn't believe she was one, but she did want to hide how much she drank.

Toward the end of her marriage, Mary was getting up in the middle of the night to have a beer and a shot. She thought this was okay because she didn't really want a drink until after work. She worked in a dental office taking X-rays and to this day doesn't understand how her appearance and behavior were ignored. After drinking the night before, Mary would go to work without brushing her teeth or bathing. She had to smell. She even passed out at work while smoking and burned a hole in the chair and through her jeans. Yes, she was embarrassed but in total denial. She didn't have a problem; her husband did.

No one ever said a word to her about her drinking and drugging. Yet she did many of the classic alcoholic things like making phone calls to everyone she knew, telling them how much she loved them, and talking about nothing. Mary and her husband stopped using LSD and mescaline because these were becoming "too adulterated," and they wanted more natural drugs. So they started using peyote and mushrooms instead. Marijuana kind of fell by the wayside, but they discovered cocaine. Coke was everything both of them wanted—the energy and the rush. Mary says she could then clean for hours, talk for hours, and still settle down at night. Cocaine also helped her drink more. The reality was, as Mary so aptly puts it, "that nothing ever got done except in my mind."

A year before she ended the marriage and moved away from her "problems," her husband went through the d.t.'s. At the hospital, he was told that his drinking was starting to affect him physically and that the d.t.'s and seizures were due to his alcoholism. "I am married to an alcoholic?"

Mary thought. She was so embarrassed that she couldn't tell anyone. She was encouraged to go to a 12-Step meeting to support her husband, but that meant she had to learn how to live with an alcoholic, and she knew she definitely was not sticking around. She sat with him while he was in detox. She fed him Valium after each grand mal seizure with a drink in her hand because *she* wasn't the alcoholic. Actually, he never did stop drinking, and so she left. She packed her belongings and moved to a city closer to her family. Before her own marriage ended, Mary's mom had remarried. He didn't drink but had had an ex-wife and daughter who did. His daughter died of alcoholism, and his ex-wife, of emphysema. He never said a word to Mary, but she found out later he was instrumental in planning an intervention.

She fed her husband Valium after each grand mal seizure with a drink in her hand because she wasn't the alcoholic.

So after she left her alcoholic husband behind, she saw no consequences at all in her own drinking and using. She carried on but was hiding the amount she drank. Her family made light drinks, and a bottle of vodka might last them a week. Mary was drinking a fifth a night. When her younger brother left for rehab, he introduced Mary to a coke dealer. Mary was living in her brother's house at the time, and when he returned from rehab, he more or less kicked her out. Her mom and stepfather moved Mary to a little house they owned. "My brother is so mean," Mary thought. "I can't be myself in his house."

Mary was now working in a different dental office and wasn't drinking as much. She didn't have to. She was using cocaine. Mary had also found a new love, crack!

She didn't stop drinking because the high from crack was only "amazing for a good ten minutes." Mary was happy.

Her life changed but not for the better. Mary fell in love with the man who taught her how to smoke crack. The fact that he was married didn't make any difference to her. What she liked was that she was a white woman and he a black man, and that made her feel bold, different, and great. She was supporting him, but then he left her. Not only did she have to find another person from whom to buy crack, but also her biggest struggle became "what was wrong with me that he left?" She started embezzling to pay for her crack, got caught, and lost her job. Mary noticed these consequences to her drinking and drugging but was able to blame them on others. Her mother paid back everything she owed, and so there were no charges. Nothing was ever said about it again.

Times, dates, consequences, and people became blurry at this point in Mary's life. What she does remember was losing a great county job, embezzling from minimarts where she worked for very short time, and another good job as a dispatcher. She slept with men she didn't know. At one point she was even held captive in someone's house (where she never paid rent because she just never paid rent). She was trying to break up with this man, and he beat her, raped her, and held her for six hours.

There was also an elderly man, in particular, who gave Mary a place to live and bought her drugs if she would sleep with him. Of course, she did. While living with the elderly man, she had a job at a drive-in hamburger place. She had actually worked herself up to manager. She ordered food supplies, scheduled five other employees, and took care of the money, too! The woman who owned this establishment was a recovering alcoholic and in a

12-Step program. Mary was confused. She was not drinking or drugging on the job, so why was this woman always talking about her life before alcohol and her life now? She even offered to take Mary to a meeting. Mary did not consider herself an alcoholic, but she was later fired from that job because of her drinking. Mary described the woman who had tried to help her as "just a bitch."

When the elderly man died, his son came out from the East Coast to sell the house. Mary slept with him, but he still threw her out. She had no place to live, so her brother told her she could live with him. After she had lost the job at the burger place, her brother told her she had to go. Again, she had no place to live.

While all of this was going on, Mary's family decided to do an intervention. She found out about this later. She was told that the entire family was going to get together for a visit. They all came, but Mary never showed. She can only say that she didn't really know anything about an intervention, but just that it wasn't convenient for her to visit her mom that day. The only thing she says she felt was a little guilt because she didn't see her brothers.

Since she had absolutely nowhere to live, her parents said Mary could move back to the house they had given her a number of years ago. Her parents owned four small houses, one of which was Mary's and another of which was empty. Mary convinced her dealer to put in an application. He had money because he didn't use. He got the house, and Mary's parents thought he was a great tenant because he always paid the rent. They didn't realize that it was a crack house. Mary was quite happy (but lonely) because she was so close to her dealer. Occasionally, he would cook it up and give her a "few rocks for the use of the house."

Then Mary found someone to fill the loneliness. Unfortunately, it was another married man sent to her house by her dealer neighbor. It seemed that this man's wife didn't use, and so he needed a refuge. It didn't take long for him to start visiting every night to smoke and have sex. He got caught for embezzlement at a job he'd had for twenty years. His family sent him to rehab to get clean and start the healing process with them. That process, which begins with the person admitting his addiction, working on and cooperating with all aspects of treatment, and the willingness to change, didn't take. Mary got him back. Although she had told him she could not get pregnant, she did. She was forty-three years old. He was still in rehab at the time.

When Mary found out that she was pregnant, she had one more night of crack and drinking. She did not stop smoking cigarettes. When her boyfriend left rehab, he stayed clean until about two weeks before their son was born. Mary found out that he was smoking again, and with a new baby, she was getting no attention from her boyfriend. She stayed clean until about three months after the birth. She had truly believed that a child of her own would keep her clean. Today she says, "I have learned that nothing matters more or can relieve the addiction until you decide you want help."

Mary started back drinking and smoking crack again exactly where she had left off, but now there was this child who felt like a burden. Mary was working on weekends and able to take the baby with her. Her boyfriend was also working. They argued more and more about money, responsibilities, friends, just about anything. One night in the middle of a screaming match, Mary's boyfriend stripped her naked, grabbed her by the hair, and pulled her down the driveway to the street. He locked her out of the house. A neighbor called the police. Mary was permitted back into the house to dress, get the baby, and was taken to the hospital. He went to jail.

If her boyfriend's family hadn't hated her enough before, now they really loathed her. Mary went to court to get the charges lifted, but at that point, it wasn't up to her. He served two weeks in jail. Mary visited every day, babe in arms, to apologize. He was also ordered to take twelve weeks of anger management. Mary believes it just made him angrier.

Mary was asked to move up to a full-time position at work, but the hangovers from the alcohol and crack were affecting her performance. She was reprimanded twice. The first time, she lied to get off the hook, and the second time, she just walked out of the job.

Her mom knew she was spiraling out of control and suggested Mary live with her. So Mary and the baby went to her mom's, and the boyfriend went to a friend's house. He would visit at times and take Mary and the baby out for a drive. A drive meant driving around and smoking crack with the windows up and the baby in the backseat.

Occasionally, Mary would go to the beach with the baby and spend the day drinking, waiting for her boyfriend to get off of work. One particular day she waited so that they could buy drugs when he was done. It didn't turn out as planned. It was dark and rainy when he left work, and instead of buying dope with Mary, he got into his own car and drove off. Mary was so angry and so drunk that she sped down a very windy road.

> A drive meant driving around and smoking crack with the windows up and the baby in the backseat.

She ended up totaling her car with her two-year-old son in the back. He was okay, but there happened to be a police officer in training behind her. She was taken to jail. This was her first brush with the law.

Shortly after, Mary, the baby, and her boyfriend moved to a rental—another property owned by her mom. The couple continued to use and fight in front of the baby. For two more years, they continued drinking, using, and fighting. Mary was arrested for domestic violence. The police took her to jail. When she was released, she came home and drank again and within twelve hours was back in jail.

Within the next ten months, Mary was arrested fifteen times. She would get released, come home, drink again, get arrested, and then the same thing again. The boyfriend finally left. At this time, Mary was not using. She was drinking, though, and even after going to jail fifteen times, she couldn't figure out how she kept getting imprisoned. The very last time she served one year in jail and finally asked for a program to help her stop drinking.

Mary was offered a one-hundred-day program where she could take her son with her. Her thinking was that she *Within the next ten months, Mary was arrested fifteen times.* "could do this for one hundred days and then get on with my life. I had no vision of what recovery looked like or any belief that I could do more than one hundred days." The first forty-five days were hell. She wanted to leave. She really thought she had enough information to stay sober but also didn't want to go back to jail.

The day finally came. It was July 14. That was the day Mary began to want what she saw in the other women in recovery. She finally surrendered after thirty-eight hard years. She got down on her knees for the first time in her life and asked for help. She had no clue what kind of help she needed or wanted. She was just done.

The recovery center gave her the structure she needed and gave her son a mother who was learning how to be a parent. She was seeing him for the very first time. After her one hundred days, Mary was given eight months of aftercare in the form of a weekly group of women who had completed residential treatment. Mary does not believe that the one hundred days would have kept her clean. It didn't seem enough time for the years she had spent in her addictions. It was the strong fellowship of the women in aftercare that Mary believes saved her life. They were amazing women, and today Mary gets to be there for them, too, if and when they call.

It was the strong fellowship of the women in aftercare that Mary believes saved her life.

Mary is not afraid to say that there have been some very hard days. But no day is worse than her best day of using. Today she lives in gratitude. She prays, journals, goes to 12-Step meetings, and has a sponsor. She had to surrender in order to get out of hell. Today, she looks around and sees the greatness of God all around her.

Chapter IV

Divine Intervention

After half a century in psychiatric practice, I know with-
out a doubt that the source of addiction is spiritual defi-
ciency. Irrespective of whether we are religious or atheist,
all human beings are spiritual by nature, and spirituality
is the cornerstone of our recovery.

—Abraham Twerski

IF YOU ARE A SPIRITUAL PERSON and/or you understand the spiritual nature of a 12-Step program, you will understand how and why a divine intervention could take place. There is nothing religious about it; it has to do with a Higher Power, and each of us has his or her own. Most of us would call our Higher Power "God," but there are some who do not. That does not mean they cannot experience a divine intervention.

A divine intervention does not mean that we see a light, hear a voice, or witness a miracle. It happens via a person or an experience. It might be better explained as someone—and not necessarily someone you know—being at the right place at the right time, or an event that brings one to a moment of clarity when nothing else could. Maybe the divine intervention is what happens within the addict's head in the midst of a struggle that could determine life or death.

The important thing to remember is that for addicts in the throes of their disease, God or a god or even anything better usually doesn't exist; they have given up.

Over and over again, we hear people in recovery share that when they could sink no deeper, when they didn't care anymore, or when they were ready to end it all, they humbly and sincerely prayed, "God, please help me"—and He did. The important thing to remember is that for addicts in the throes of their disease, God or a god or even anything better usually doesn't exist; we have given up.

When an addict pleads for help, and it comes in some way, shape, or form—whether it be a person or situation—that is considered divine. When an addict opens his eyes and declares he wants to be free of his disease and seriously seeks recovery, that could also be called divine. In recovery we might refer to these as "God shots" or something similar. All that really means is something greater than ourselves opened a door for us, and we acknowledged that. It is anyone's personal interpretation if an intervention was divine. No one can tell another it was not. Divine intervention comes from the soul. Since recovery is not something we can undertake on our own, it is spiritually enlightening to believe that the intervention was divine and then the humans took over!

I believe that every single addict who recovers has a moment of divine intervention somewhere within her history. When you read the stories in this chapter, you will see how and when a divine intervention took place, even if shows up in just a small event. Those of us in recovery and who work the 12 Steps know that "no human power could have relieved our alcoholism" or any of the other addictions we suffer.

God works in mysterious ways!

Kathy

I would love to have a sense of serenity all of the time, but I don't. I know only that the difference between peace and serenity is that peace seems to come from my heart, but serenity is when my soul smiles.

—Kathy L.

I'm not sure if I could tell you exactly how I got to the point where my drinking became a way of life. I lived to dread every day because no matter what I tried to tell myself, today would be exactly like the day before and the day before that and the day before that. I now know this is called "insanity."

Like most alcoholics (although I did not think of myself as such), I tried the self-help books, meditation classes, and anything else that would offer me a reprieve from my disease. I wanted hope that tomorrow would be different. But it never was. Today I hear other alcoholics share how they would stay

> *"I lived to dread every day because no matter what I tried to tell myself, today would be exactly like the day before and the day before that and the day before that."*

sober for a day or week or month, and I am still in awe. I drank every single day (for how long I don't know), and my drinking day began at 8:00 a.m.

Oddly enough, no one ever told me to quit drinking. Once or twice something might have been mentioned, but I did not experience the pleading, begging, and crying I have seen family members resort to in order to convince a loved one to get help. My bottom came when I could no longer manipulate anyone and I was about to lose everything and everyone in my life.

To hold my life together and to make sure it was obvious I was trying (I played the victim well), I called a 12-Step recovery group. I didn't know anything about the organization and didn't know anyone in it. My call was answered by a man who went by "Joseph." He asked me a few questions, including if I had been drinking that day. The answer to that was, of course, yes. He asked me to meet him the following day for coffee, and he would take me to a 12-Step meeting. He also had only one request, and that was not to take one more drink for the remainder of the day. It was only late morning, but I promised him. I did not have any more to drink. The day was December 10.

"My bottom came when I could no longer manipulate anyone and I was about to lose everything and everyone in my life."

I anxiously and nervously met Joseph on December 11. I had kept my promise not to have a drink. I attended my first 12-Step recovery meeting; got a twenty-four-hour sobriety chip, my Big Book; and I've never had to take a drink since. I thanked Joseph from the bottom of my heart. He did not attend meetings in my area, so I called him when I celebrated thirty days of sobriety and also sixty days. I never saw Joseph again until . . .

Sobriety brought my next big addiction to the forefront: that demon nicotine! Throughout the years, my family did plead and beg on this front, and my daughter would write me letters telling me how much she would miss me if I died. My husband would get angry at the prospect that I could get ill from something that could be avoided. In many ways, nicotine was a worse enemy to me than alcohol. I had tried a million times to stop, yet I gave in over and over again. I admired those who could quit but figured there was no way I could.

My moment of clarity came, and I could see that life might be better and certainly healthier if I stopped smoking. With the help of what I had learned from the 12 Steps and the successes I saw in others who had stopped, I decided to pick a day to quit. The day was January 11. It was my grandmother's birthday, and she had died at the age of ninety-five on the same day. That meant something to me. The plan was to pick up the "patch" the night before after one of my regular 12-Step meetings.

The evening of January 10 (these dates are important), the night before I would quit, I went to my meeting. There was a guy there I had never seen at this meeting before. I kept staring at him. When he introduced himself to the group, he said his name was Joseph. *My* Joseph? I still wasn't sure. It was way too much of a coincidence. But then nothing is really a coincidence: A coincidence is my Higher Power's plan for me. I couldn't wait for the meeting to end. I immediately approached Joseph and asked him if he remembered me. He said he

"A coincidence is my Higher Power's plan for me."

did. We spoke for a minute or two before I left. I picked up my nicotine patch and stopped smoking January 11. I have been smoke-free for a number of years now, and I have not seen or heard from Joseph since that night.

Sometimes I tell this story, and someone will say, "Gee, eleven must be your lucky number!" Or they just don't get the fact that this guy, a complete stranger in my life, had to have been sent by God. I thought then, and still do today, that God must have thought that Joseph worked out so well for me with my alcohol addiction, why not send him to me again?

"You may be only one person in the world, but you may be the world to one person."

There is a quote that I love, and when I hear it, I think of Joseph: "You may be only one person in the world, but you may be the world to one person." Thank you, God, and thank you, Joseph!

Chapter V

After Intervention, or the Decision to Recover

Just 'cause you got the monkey off your back doesn't mean the circus has left town.

—George Carlin

M Y HUSBAND HAD A BUSINESS acquaintance whose son was a drug addict. The acquaintance had moved to our area with his wife and daughter, but the son remained in the Midwest. The man was open about going to bring his twenty-something-year-old son to be with them in the hopes that he would get help. It was very unlike my husband to talk about my journey into recovery, but he did and asked his friend if he wanted me to call him. He said he did and asked if I would speak with his wife also. We talked, and I believed the father was on the right track. The mom was not going to get on board but was "done" to some extent.

A few months ago, and about a year since I had talked to them, I got a frantic phone call. It was late, but I answered *because* it was late. It was the mom. The son had stolen money from his sister, the sister had called the police, and they were on their way. He was high. Now whether this was the right or wrong thing is not for me to judge, but the mom did not want him arrested. She wanted him somewhere safe. Her reason for calling me was to ask where he could go.

Well, the problem was I didn't know. If I had had time to sit and think and plan and call people, I could have helped her better. I did suggest a few places, but when she called them, they would not take him because he was high and needed medical assistance. At that point, I told her to take him to the nearest ER. I honestly don't know what happened after that. All I do know is that the father told my husband that he and his wife were divorcing after more than twenty-five years of marriage. I'm not surprised.

So the purpose of this chapter is to give you information on the recovery process along the same lines that would have helped the mom in this story. There are choices, and if you are a family member, you might want to begin understanding what avenues are available. If you are the addicted person and have made the decision to recover, this will also help you. This is general information and geared primarily toward the alcoholic/substance abuser. While every addict can have a formal, informal, or divine intervention, there are nuances to some addictions such as gambling and sex that make the decision to recover a bit different than for the alcoholic or drug abuser. (We'll talk about some of these later on in this chapter.)

I cannot recommend any facility or any particular interventionist, therapist, or counselor by name. So let's just begin at the point when the family determines a formal intervention is in order. This will lessen the burden because the interventionist will be there as a guide and will recommend where the addict might go to detox, rehab, or IOP therapy. The family should, of course, get firsthand information about where their loved one might go and be ready to ask any questions. Chapter II on formal interventions covers this subject more in detail.

If there will *not* be a formal intervention, the addict and family (or sometimes only the addict) might make a solo decision that a residential inpatient treatment facility should be the first step toward recovery. There are countless residential inpatient treatment facilities online these days, and every one sounds and looks like a vacation spot. In fact, there is so much information online it makes your head spin. Many can be reached by an 800 number, which for some reason doesn't sit well with me. It reminds me of a call center where someone rings a bell when they get a good "hit." The list of resources at the end of this book provides a good starting point to do research and learn more on your own about addiction and organizations that might be helpful. You can call any of these (most have someone on call twenty-four hours a day) for information. You can also read the literature these groups publish online. Most of these organizations, however, will not recommend a treatment facility, but some may suggest one that is familiar to them. The wisest thing is to find a good counselor or therapist who understands the particular addiction and can make a recommendation. Of course, they will want to see the addicted person to assess the situation, but this is a good thing. Many of the people I know in recovery made a decision to stop their addiction, saw a counselor who was recommended to them, and got help finding the proper rehab facility based on their situation and financial means. Remember, these places are not one-size-fits-all. Residential inpatient facilities can cost upward of $50,000 for ninety days, while others cost nothing or next to nothing. Most fall somewhere in the middle. Residential inpatient programs are generally expensive, and because of that, they will accept insurance.

Remember that insurance companies are not all the same in terms of coverage. Scott Peterson, MA, LMFT, LICAC, director of an outpatient facility, explained to me that some insurance companies do not want to invest in the highest level of care first, that is, residential inpatient treatment. Even if addicts may require this level, an insurance company might prefer they try an outpatient program first. Is this prolonging the recovery process? Does it possibly set this person up to fail in recovery? Not necessarily; sometimes outpatient *is* enough, and if it is a matter of insurance and money, that may be the only alternative.

Residential inpatient treatment facilities may not have the medical staff to handle and monitor detox on-site, but even if they are not connected with a facility, they can still recommend where the addict can go prior to inpatient. These facilities do not accept a person who is still drinking or drugging. Today, most recovery centers work with the entire person. They assess the individual; offer individual and group counseling sessions; mandate 12-Step meetings; provide meditation groups, yoga, and other exercise; oversee nutrition and diet; and, most important, if you don't follow the rules, you still can go. Most offer family weekends and family programs. As I mentioned earlier in chapter II, family members sometimes attend the same residential inpatient facility as the addicted person, although certainly not the same program and not at the same time. Recovery centers encompass a variety of programs ranging from one week to months. Some facilities offer aftercare programs, and most have an "alumni" organization that sends out newsletters or offers activities for continuous support.

Without the assistance of a professional, you may be tempted to choose a residential facility for the ambience. Yes, many of them are unbelievably beautiful! This is not to say that these not great recovery centers, but don't underestimate programs offered by the Salvation Army and others in your area that might not be as "high end." I have known people who have gone to both the most expensive and the least expensive facilities in the United States, and at the end of the day, it has been up to the individual how she works that recovery program and stays on track.

Intensive outpatient (IOP) programs are considered the next level of care. There are definitely reasons why one would choose an IOP program, the biggest being financial. As I mentioned before, insurance companies may be more willing to pay for an IOP program than a higher level of care. Most IOP programs provide individual counseling, group counseling, relapse prevention, and other educational activities. The IOP group might meet three times a week for three hours a day for a period of six to eight weeks. The word "intensive" should tell you that they are extremely focused. The client lives in his own home and, depending on the nature and hours of employment, could continue a "normal" life.

The next level of care is outpatient (OP) programs. OP programs vary greatly. They usually take up less time per day/per week, but the actual length of the process may be up to twelve months. There are some organizations that work with various levels of OP programs. The National Council on Alcoholism and Drug Dependence (NCADD) in my area offers great women's programs and works in levels. Level 1 is all about education and groups; Level 2 digs a bit deeper and focuses on core issues such as family, trauma, abuse; and Level 3 is aftercare and an ongoing weekly group meeting providing tools for day-to-day recovery.

Outpatient programs (and some IOP programs) can be found under "behavioral health services" and "counseling services" in the Yellow Pages or online. Some of these have sliding scale fees, and some are nonprofit.

There are fabulous women's recovery centers in all part of the United States that offer a phenomenal menu of services. These are especially valuable to addict mothers with children. These programs offer counseling on women's issues, parenting groups, prenatal education, nutrition, midwives, spirituality and meditation groups, yoga, skills building, resume writing, vocational counseling, GED prep, and there could possibly be more! Many of these also have living facilities where these moms can stay with their children for a period of time.

Anyone who has been in any type of treatment for an addiction could choose to live in a halfway house/sober-living environment. I would ask for a recommendation from your treatment facility, and in many cases you must reserve your bed. These are extremely helpful for people who need more time to learn how to live sober out there in the world today. They vary in many ways depending on location, but the bottom line to all of them is that it's all about sobriety, and so, as difficult as it may be to get a bed, it is just as easy to be asked to leave if you disobey the house rules.

If all this sounds confusing and daunting, it can be. The important thing is to know what options are out there whether you decide to do something today or tomorrow or next week. My personal advice is if you are an addict or have an addicted loved one in your life, get to it immediately.

There isn't an addict in this world who just wakes up one morning, says "I'm done!" and walks away from the addiction a new person. If you have heard the term "dry drunk," it refers to an addict who isn't using whatever the drug of choice was any longer but has not changed emotionally, psychologically, and spiritually. Most of the time, these are rather miserable people. They suffer and make everyone around them suffer because they can't have what it is they want. These people, if they are willing, could change their lives considerably if they involved themselves in a 12-Step program. Keep in mind that addictions are a symptom of a deeper problem, so merely not drinking, drugging, gambling, etc. isn't enough to truly change a person.

Addictions are a symptom of a deeper problem, so merely not drinking, drugging, gambling, etc. isn't enough to truly change a person.

Addiction professionals know this. They understand that there has to be something to keep a person sober ("sober," by the way, is used to indicate a person is "clean" of any addiction). There are 12-Step programs for every type of addiction, and the majority of residential, IOP, and OP programs and counseling and behavioral centers, even sober-living facilities, structure recovery around the 12 Steps. Facilities may not have meetings on their premises, but meetings may be a requirement of the program.

A large number of addiction professionals are in recovery. They know addiction firsthand, and I have not met one of them who has ever stayed sober without working a solid 12-Step program. They, in turn, strongly recommend that their patients attend meetings, get a sponsor, and work the steps. There is a saying in the fellowship: "It works if you work it." There will always be naysayers who feel it didn't work for them or who know someone for whom it didn't work. My personal experience is that if you truly want to remain sober, you will involve yourself in a 12-Step program. It is by far the strongest support system you can have, regardless of family and friends. Why? Because you are surrounded by folks exactly like you! The same goes for 12-Step meetings for families—and there are a variety of different programs for families. As one counselor told me, the peer support comes first, and the behavioral intervention is second. Knowing you have a group of like-minded people behind you begins to change the way you think and live.

Knowing you have a group of like-minded people behind you begins to change the way you think and live.

I am one of those people who did not receive any formal type of recovery therapy. One day I picked up the phone, called the 12-Step recovery number, and haven't looked back since. There is no "norm" for recovery, but I am probably in the minority. If you *think* you are addicted or that a loved one is addicted, you don't need permission to attend an "open" meeting. ("Closed" meetings, on the other hand, are restricted to the addicts themselves.) You don't have to say a word. You can literally be a fly on the wall and listen. No one forces you to do anything you do not want to do. There are no dues or fees. The only requirement for a 12-Step program is a desire to stop an addiction and to be willing to do whatever it takes.

Twelve-Step programs are offered worldwide. No matter where you are around the globe, you can stop in at a meeting and know you belong. All people in 12-Step recovery speak the same language, and it is one of understanding and compassion.

I am a 12-Step program cheerleader, and I could go on and on and on about what it has done for me and what I have seen it do for countless others who felt hopeless and in total despair. All the people who share their stories in this book have achieved sobriety and have remained sober while working a 12-Step program.

Information about any of these programs can be found online. The location, time, and type of meeting will be listed. A meeting could be a women's meeting, a men's meeting, a speaker meeting, or a meeting that reads and discusses the Steps or other relevant literature. Not all meetings are perfect for everyone, but there is always one that will fit comfortably in every way.

Residential treatment, IOP and OP programs, counseling, therapy, and any other services that mark the beginning of recovery are invaluable. They are first steps, each of which comes to a conclusion. Recovery is a lifelong process, and addicts require something that will take them through the ups and downs of the real world. That's where 12-Step recovery programs come in.

These are simple programs for complicated people. As it says in "How It Works" in The Big Book, "Rarely have we seen a person fail who has thoroughly followed our path."

Recovery requires time and patience on the part of the addict as well as on the part of the family and friends of the addict. No one aspires to be or dreams of the day they can stand up and say, for example, "My name is Kathy, and I am an alcoholic." Recovery is difficult. There are a hundred things on a daily basis (at least in the beginning of the recovery process) that can make a person wonder if recovery is the answer. It is.

No matter where you are around the globe, you can stop in at a meeting and know you belong.

I am hopeful that the information here will give you a much better idea of the types of assistance out there to help you or a loved one recover. The resource section at the end of this book lists websites I feel are important. Check them out, and go a step further, opening up the links you find there. Look for online meetings. One note of caution, though: There are quite a few blogs on recovery sites, so remember what you read in them is only someone's opinion. Be wary of advice from someone who does not know your situation, especially if it involves an addicted family member. Most of us can only speak from our own experiences. So taking advice from laypeople may not always be in the addict's or the family's best interest; that's where the broader experience of the professional counselor comes in.

Still, no matter where recovery begins or who is involved, there is something that never changes, and that is you have to take it "one day at a time!"

Characteristics of Other Addictions

At the beginning of this chapter, I mentioned that there were some differences in addictions and how they might be approached and the steps to recovery, the first being gambling. I had the privilege of speaking to Rick Benson, the director of Algamus Recovery Centers. Rick is a nationally certified gambling counselor with twenty-three years of experience. Rick gave me quite a bit of insight into compulsive gambling, and I am going to highlight some of the nuances so that you might better understand this addiction and the recovery process.

First of all, gambling could be called the "invisible addiction." You can still look good on the outside as opposed to how alcoholics, drug abusers, and those with eating disorders tend to deteriorate physically.

There are a hundred things on a daily basis (at least in the beginning of the recovery process) that can make a person wonder if recovery is the answer. It is.

Most people think that the compulsive gambler is usually male, but that is not true. The number of female compulsive gamblers is on the rise. It is also an addiction that hits the twenty-year-old who becomes obsessed with poker as well as the senior citizen who can't get enough of the slots.

The compulsive gambler goes through three different phases of addiction, and most do not seek recovery until they are at the last stage: desperation. That is when the consequences have built up, and for many, this is only after a number of years. The interesting thing about gambling is that the alcoholic knows the next pint of whiskey won't solve his problems and the crack addict knows that the next rock won't solve her problems, but the compulsive gambler lives in the delusion that the next big win will make it all okay. There is a financial bottom that is geometrically deeper for the compulsive gambler than for any other addict. The seriousness of this disease is reflected in the fact that the incidence of attempted suicide is five times higher for gambling addicts than for any other addiction and fourteen times higher than in the general populace.

The alcoholic knows the next pint of whiskey won't solve his problems and the crack addict knows that the next rock won't solve her problems, but the compulsive gambler lives in the delusion that the next big win will make it all okay.

Rick told me that if you are a compulsive gambler, you have about a 35 to 40 percent chance of developing a drug and/or alcohol addiction. This is important to know when you are trying to find a recovery center, and it affects how the insurance company will handle it. Most insurance companies will not pay for residential treatment for a compulsive gambler. Some insurance companies will pay for OP programs, but most will not unless there is another addiction present. Compulsive gamblers (like most addicts) are often dual or even poly-addicted. So if you are a gambler/alcoholic, or a cocaine user/gambler, you may be able to get into treatment based on the addiction other than gambling.

A formal intervention is possible, but the compulsive gambler is usually in big denial. A compulsive gambler does not identify herself with alcoholics or drug abusers because she usually believes she is better than that. As Rick describes them, they are "somewhat narcissistic, excessively entitled addicts" that can't see themselves as "down-and-out."

So how does a compulsive gambler begin recovery? By talking to a counselor who, like Rick, knows this addiction inside and out. Gambling-specific residential treatment centers like Algamus will accept alcoholics or drug addicts if the person meets a pathological gambling diagnosis. Residential treatment can last thirty to seventy days, and as for any addiction, the longer the better. These programs involve group therapy, individual therapy, 12-Step meetings, and even a health club membership. After residential treatment, OP counseling and 12-Step programs are recommended.

We talk constantly about family involvement, and here is where compulsive gambling is also different. This is a family disease like all the rest. In 12-Step programs for the families of alcoholics, we learn it is important to detach with love from the alcoholic; the important thing for families of compulsive gamblers who are in a 12-Step program is that they may have to detach in anger, but they *must* detach. It is difficult for the gambler to have a spouse take control of the money in the household; and there are ten states that are community property states. This means that the spouse is civilly liable for all of the gambler's criminal and civil debt, and it is pretty hard to detach with love while all this is getting piled on. It makes the treatment process much longer regardless of whether the addict starts with residential treatment or not.

Rick believes that gamblers are only drug addicts who don't ingest a drug. The dopamine levels in the brain rise to an elevated state while gambling and then crash when the money is lost. Compulsive gambling has never had a poster child, so to speak. They have not had a Betty Ford who would make people stand up and take notice. Many people still have the misconception that a gambling problem is a moral weakness. People thought the same of alcoholics many years ago. Hopefully, the information Rick has given us will be of benefit to many of you who are questioning your gambling habits or those of a loved one. I have included the website for Algamus as well as 12-Step programs for gamblers and their families in the resources section at the back of this book.

Many people still have the misconception that a gambling problem is a moral weakness.

The second addiction that has a few differences in intervention and recovery is sex addiction. This one is difficult for many people to grasp because a sex addiction is not the same as having a high appetite for sex. A sex addiction is shame based, and that is the core component. Jeff Schultz, a certified sex-addiction therapist, was willing to talk to me about this "newest" addiction that has been brought to our attention via the lives of the rich and famous.

Like gambling, it is not one of those addictions recognizable by anyone from the outside. The sexual behaviors are kept secret, yet the spouse of a sex addict often feels that something isn't right, and the sex addict is in denial. Sex addiction is consistent with other addictions in that the addict experiences being out of control. The behaviors may work for a while, but then the intensity changes. An example would be that instead of looking at *Playboy*, the addict would have to find a much more intense source of porn. There is an escalation.

Sex addiction affects the family, as does any other addiction. Jeff says that he sees more and more people in relationships who have offended that relationship and are facing breakup, divorce, or loss of custody and relationships with their children.

It may be twelve to thirteen years before an addict comes to Jeff. Sobriety for the sex addict is different than sobriety for an alcoholic. You can't just say "Stop!" As Jeff says, "This drug lives between someone's ears, so they can get a fix anytime." Sexuality is not a bad thing, but the sex addict misuses it. There are interventions a sex addict needs to make to be okay in the short term. A decision or crisis stage, pangs of conscience, marriage trouble, or some type of a bottom that looks like the addiction has been discovered is the impetus for recovery.

Sex addiction affects the family just as any other addiction.

Therapy is usually the first part of recovery for the sex addict. It is important to work with a therapist, because unlike for other addictions, there needs to be a "disclosure," an honest exposure of what has been going on. The addict must define a bottom-line set of behaviors that he will identify as out of control and addictive. It becomes the core set of behaviors. Sexual sobriety does not mean a person will stay celibate forever; that is not natural. What the therapist will recommend is abstinence for a time as the person learns to be sexual in a healthy way. There are no rigid rules.

Residential rehab is recommended if someone is struggling with this addiction and having a difficult time putting two or three days of sobriety together. There are residential treatment centers in many parts of the country that work with a large sex addiction population. Few are dedicated only to sex addiction. To assist in the therapy, the patient may be placed in an IOP program or workshops better known as "retreats." A good number of spouses of sex addicts attend workshops and spend time in residential treatment centers also. The family is a very important part of the recovery dynamic. Jeff feels that having the support of one's family is a good reason to turn the ship around, so to speak.

Sex addiction afflicts men and women. I asked Jeff if it could be uncomfortable for a female client to work with a male therapist. He says it is not uncomfortable, once the proverbial ice is broken. I mention this because it is important that you can feel comfortable with your therapist.

If you feel you have a sex addiction, you should find a therapist who concentrates on this area. Because so much of the behavior is secret, it may be difficult for anyone, even a spouse, to be sure that a partner *is* a sex addict. In Jeff's practice, he begins with a formal assessment that will give him information and data about the person's relationship to sex. He also uses an index to measure the relationship of stress, money, and work. You may wonder what these have to do with sex. Jeff explained to me that asking questions that assess the whole person provides clues about any other compulsions that may be important to the diagnosis of an addiction. He asks about drug or alcohol history and the relationship

If you feel you have a sex addiction, you should find a therapist who concentrates on this area.

of any chemicals to sex. He feels that his clients tend to be honest by this time because they are in crisis. Many times a person doesn't really understand sex addiction but just knows something is not right. All these assessments help Jeff walk the client through to a better understanding.

The difficult part of sex addiction is opening up to a spouse who is now learning of all the behaviors for the first time. It is especially important that the couple work with a therapist so that both can heal. Often spouses ends up with all the anger because they can never get over what was done and do not want to risk staying in the relationship. I find it interesting that Jeff says that sex addiction is an "intimacy-killing disorder. It is about risk. It's not about trust, because the trust has been destroyed."

Sex addiction is a real disease. Like gambling, it is often misjudged as a person having no self-control. Many believe it is just a cop-out for those who want to do what they wish sexually and then blame it on an addiction. It is not just about sex, but also power and control. It (like gambling) has no spokesperson or role model standing up for recovery, if you will, but the hope is that understanding for this disease will gain momentum just as alcoholism had in the 1930s.

Every addiction has a 12-Step program. Jeff believes it is very important for sex addicts to be a part of one. They may also continue therapy for as long as they and their therapist feel it is contributing to their sobriety. I have included Jeff's website in the resources section as well as a site for 12-Step programs for sex addiction. Jeff has some excellent information on his site for both men and women.

The next topic, love addiction, is probably the most difficult for me to describe because it is based on such an intangible human need—love. Oddly enough, though, it isn't about love at all but rather relationships. It acts in opposition to real love and genuine intimacy. It looks like love, but it is based on dependencies, low self-esteem, and abandonment issues.

Love addiction is not the same as sex addiction. Yes, a person can be addicted to both, but then, many addicts are addicted to more than one thing. There is a 12-Step recovery program that combines both sex and love, but there is also one for love addicts only. I called upon Jeff Schultz again for information on this addiction because he treats love addicts as well and was a student of Pia Mellody, who is well-known for her work in codependency and love addiction.

The basis of love addiction, according to Jeff, is when one person makes another person an object of fantasy. It is an obsession with another person, and the love addict cannot find any fault in the person they love and may project unrealistic characteristics onto that person. The "beloved" can do no wrong. He will deny any shortfalls in his beloved and make excuses to others for this person and his/her behaviors.

The basis of love addiction is abandonment. Jeff uses the example of a five-year-old being left on the side of the road all alone: totally helpless and afraid and feeling that he could die if someone doesn't come to the rescue.

Abandonment issues begin in childhood. In heterosexual adults, abandonment issues develop in father-daughter or mother-son relationships when the parent fails to provide the love and support the child needs.

The child is not a priority, and so this shames the child into believing he is worthless. Since the child's needs are neglected, the child is afraid of not being able to care for himself and as an adult believes he needs someone *else* to take care of him.

Culturally, according to Jeff, there are more women love addicts than men, as abandonment occurs more frequently on the part of fathers (whether actual abandonment or only the perception of abandonment that accompanies absences due to work). Love addicts can be great enablers because it makes them feel needed. At times, however, the reality of the beloved bursts through the obsession, and everything falls apart. There is also an opposite facet of love addiction called love avoidance. Love avoidance is the need to take care of someone else while being careful to avoid intimacy.

According to the 12-Step recovery group for love addiction, there are many types of love addicts, but the common denominator is this: "Love addicts crave an emotional connection and will avoid at any cost separation, anxiety, and loneliness."

Jeff tells me that treating the love addict is not easy. This individual does not seek therapy until there is a shattering event (like a beloved leaving) and the addict faces withdrawal, which can feel like a death has occurred. The addict can be suicidal. The process of recovery demands working on boundaries and fears of abandonment. Love addicts have difficulty with recovery work. Recovery is slow, and there is the very real danger of the addict focusing on a new "love" during the recovery process and beginning the addiction cycle all over again.

There certainly are many more addictions, but the next most obvious to me is food. Eating disorders are much more common than many people think, and you'll read some examples of food addiction situations in the stories that follow. These disorders are extremely dangerous, and professional help is a must. I am not a professional on addictions, but I have to say that I don't know anyone who voluntarily went into treatment for an eating disorder. Alcohol and food, yes; drugs and food, yes; but it was the alcohol or the drugs that came to the forefront while the food disorder was still denied. The food addict is in as much denial as an alcoholic, drug abuser, gambler, or sex addict. Unlike with gambling or sex addiction, eating disorders can sometimes be obvious to others, but not always. As in sex addiction, there are a lot of secrets. Some residential treatment centers specifically treat those suffering from anorexia and bulimia. Eating disorders cannot be dealt with like other addictions because of the fragility of the addict, physically and emotionally. Parents should take measures immediately and seek professional help if they suspect a problem.

If you are suffering from any of the addictions I have mentioned or have a loved one who you believe is suffering, you can be instrumental in some way, shape, or form in beginning the process of healing. Recovery takes patience, but there is light at *Recovery takes* the end of the tunnel. Addicts *patience, but there* cannot be cured, and just *is light at the end* because they are not drinking, *of the tunnel.* drugging, gambling, having unhealthy sex, starving, bingeing, or purging does not mean they are well. Addicts must change almost every aspect of their lives in terms of how they think and what they say and do. Even when addicts do change, others around them may not. Sobriety doesn't mean everyone lives happily ever after in the same relationships as before. But if each person takes care of him- or herself, addict or family member, everyone can live happily ever after in the kind of life they choose to live.

May God bless you and keep you.

Chapter VI

The Stories

We are going to know a new freedom and a new hap-
piness. We will not regret the past nor wish to shut the
door on it. We will comprehend the word "serenity," and
we will know peace. No matter how far down the scale
we have gone, we will see how our experience can benefit
others. That feeling of uselessness and self-pity will dis-
appear. We will lose interest in selfish things and gain
interest in our fellows. Self-seeking will slip away. Our
whole attitude and outlook upon life will change. Fear of
people and of economic insecurity will leave us. We will
intuitively know how to handle situations which used to
baffle us. We will suddenly realize that God is doing for
us what we could not do for ourselves.

—*Alcoholics Anonymous: The Big Book*

THESE WORDS, KNOWN AS THE "Promises," speak for
each person who shared a story with me. They can
vouch for how the Promises have come true in their lives

today as the result of 12-Step program recovery after years of addiction. No one graduates from recovery, and no addict is ever cured. The good news is that there is hope and a solution for every addict and family member. I am the storyteller in most of the narratives that follow, but there are a few in a different format. All the names have been changed to respect the anonymity of each person.

It is my hope that these stories will speak to you and that you will appreciate the sincere honesty of each addict who shared. There are many addicts who do not want to share their stories with so many through this type of venue. But these people have chosen to give back to the community for the gift of sobriety that each has received by describing their experiences in addiction and how they recovered. All had interventions, and no two were the same.

Dr. Wayne Dyer has said, "Once you believe in yourself and see your soul as divine and precious, you will automatically become a being who can create a miracle." This is exactly what these people have done, and each life is a miracle. All things are possible with God.

Nicole

To get something you never had, you have to do something you never did. When God takes something from your grasp, He's not punishing you, but merely opening your hands to receive something better. The will of God will never take you where the grace of God will not protect you.

—Anonymous

Nicole is a thirty-two-year-old divorced woman with shared custody of her five-year-old son. She is employed as an RN, and her drug of choice was cocaine.

Not unlike many people her age, her parents divorced when she was about three. Nicole lived primarily with her mom and visited her dad on Sundays but doesn't remember the times when they were all together. She isn't really sure if there are any alcoholics in the family but says she was exposed to "quite a bit of drunkenness as a child" through the actions of her parents and a few of her uncles.

At thirteen she took her first drink. Actually, it was much more than a drink since she kept downing beer because she didn't feel drunk. By the time she stopped, it was way too late; she blacked out and vomited for two days. She didn't drink again for another year or two.

In ninth grade she was suspended along with seven of her friends for drinking before a school dance. They weren't falling-over drunk, but thought they were being cool for breaking the rules. It was a shock to their parents and to many others because this group of kids was on student council and also participated in sports. This incident is significant to Nicole because it was the first time she had "gotten into trouble" due to her drinking.

With high school Nicole was exposed to marijuana. She had started smoking cigarettes around that time but was a little shy about pot. Oddly enough, she found it smelled familiar, and she realized that her dad's apartment had had the exact same odor! She hadn't thought to ask him about it and never told him she knew until she was in recovery. Her friends were having so much fun passing around joints that she thought she would try it. She did, and then all she wanted to do was sleep. Nicole decided that pot just wasn't her thing and would only take a hit every now and then.

Drinking, however, became a part of every party. Nicole would do shot after shot until she blacked out.

On her senior trip, she drank so much she thought she had alcohol poisoning. She vomited for two straight days. Her friends started to call an ambulance, but by that time she felt better and began to drink again. The same thing happened years later at her bachelorette party, but this time the paramedics did make an appearance. They gave her fluids, which made her feel well enough to do it all again the next night.

Not everyone can recall the turning point in their addiction, but Nicole can. She had failed a course in her nursing program, which forced her to sit out for the summer and retake it in the fall. She was so depressed she cried for days. A close friend, Renee, who always came up with wild, adventurous ideas, proposed they get out of the Midwest and head south. Nicole was not much of a risk taker, but there was a place to stay, and so the young women figured they would get jobs on the beach and have some summer fun. A week later, they were on their way.

It didn't take them long to get hired at a beach bar where the girls wore bikinis to work. This was pure culture shock to Nicole. They were invited out with a few of their coworkers who even had a limo lined up. When they arrived, one of the guys asked them if they were "rolling tonight." The two girls had no idea what he was talking about and became even more curious when the others tried to hush him up. It turned out "rolling" was the lingo for getting high on Ecstasy. Nicole and Renee decided to try it. They were a bit frightened at the effects in the beginning, but Nicole says, "It was my first of many all-nighters, and I loved every minute of it."

She couldn't wait to "roll" again, and opportunities came along frequently. They had friends from their hometown visit and introduced them to Ecstasy, but Nicole didn't think anyone loved it as much as she did. Every time she took it, she couldn't wait until the next time. Typical of any addict trying to catch that feeling first experienced with drugs or alcohol, Nicole started taking two to three pills a night to stay high, but she couldn't recapture that initial response.

When they returned home, she was drinking almost every weekend and wishing for Ecstasy. Fortunately for Nicole, it migrated north behind them and quickly became popular. Nicole was a free spirit and could be outgoing and talk with anyone. She made new friends who had access to it, and it was like the days of summer all over again.

Nicole was obsessed with nightlife. Her close friends noticed that she was getting too thin. When invited out with these friends or to family gatherings, if she showed up at all, it would be late and she would be hungover. Everyone tried to talk to her about it. Even Renee tried to talk to her, but Nicole shrugged it all off. She did not have a problem. She was having fun, and they *She did not have a problem. She was having fun, and they just didn't understand her anymore.* just didn't understand her anymore. Ecstasy was on its way out of Nicole's life anyway. Her boyfriend, who had stopped himself, convinced her to quit as well, and the police were raiding more clubs and parties. Nicole was paranoid.

She finished nursing school and kind of got back to her pre-Ecstasy self, but the beach was on her mind. Every weekend was still for drinking, and now there was a Vicodin here and there. Nicole found that alcohol and Vicodin don't mix. She took one before drinking and ended up on the floor of a restaurant. An ambulance was called, and it all amounted to a quick visit to the ER and a lot of embarrassment.

There are always things people say they would never do, addicts or not. Nicole did not ever think she would snort anything up her nose. Never say never! Her boyfriend's friend had cocaine on him one night instead of Vicodin. Nicole tried it and liked it. They snorted coke on a few other occasions, and after one of those times, she was told it wasn't coke but meth. Nicole said she was totally freaked out ... for about five seconds. Meth seemed much more dangerous than coke; still she snorted another line.

There was a temporary halt to the drugs, but the drinking continued throughout her late twenties. She didn't have a problem; it was just a phase. So she got married and had a son a year later. She and her husband were happy and had fun. They went to bars occasionally. Nicole did have a bit of postpartum depression and was given an antidepressant. She thought she was just moody.

Her husband went back to college when their son turned two. Nicole had tried to mentally prepare herself for his not being able to work if he were in school full-time. Nothing, however, forewarned her about what her life would really be like. She was working full-time and had to drop off and pick up their son at the babysitter's house. Handling a toddler, bills, and what seemed like absolutely everything in their lives was overwhelming. The depression came back with a vengeance, and so she started seeing a counselor through an employee-assistance program.

Nicole was feeling neglected and abandoned by her husband. She couldn't handle all this, and it was his fault. They spent less time together and fought more. After one of their big arguments, she went out with a friend and told him she would be staying elsewhere that night. He knew she needed to get away, and so he didn't argue with her. Nicole isn't quite sure what came over her that night, but after five years, she was craving cocaine like never before. She had no connections but made a few calls. Success! She snorted coke all night long while she reminisced about her earlier life.

She went home the next day as if nothing had changed. She didn't tell her husband about the coke. He wouldn't understand; he had never been into that scene. Anyway, it was an isolated incident and it was over—until a few weeks later when she went out with a few friends (again sans husband), and it seemed like another perfect opportunity. She now had the dealer's direct phone number. It was another all-nighter of snorting coke in the bathroom.

The cycle had begun. Nicole had saved a bit of coke for a "rainy day," and that day came the following weekend. It wasn't enough, so she called her dealer. She was now doing it alone and getting larger quantities each time. She began snorting at work. It gave her so much energy that she was getting more and more accomplished every day. So she started doing it in the morning. No one knew. It was her secret. When she was home, she could get the house cleaned, take care of the toddler, and tolerate her husband's negligence. They didn't argue as much. She had found the solution!

Nicole was still seeing a counselor and a psychiatrist for her depression. She was also on Ativan for anxiety attacks. She was hiding the coke from her husband, so she had to figure out a way to make all this work. She would use Ativan to counteract the cocaine so she could sleep when she was high. If they went out for dinner, she would make trips to the ladies' room to snort a line or two. The coke made her drink more beer, and so no one thought twice about why she was high. Her husband thought she was doing great. Later on he couldn't believe that he could have been so dumb. Nicole had always handled the money, and so he never knew how much was missing or how broke they were.

Nicole needed cocaine to get her moving in the morning and to keep her going all day. She didn't think anyone knew what she was doing, but there were some concerns. Most everyone thought she was just sinking back into her depression. Her mom had even consulted with Renee privately, and they were both watching Nicole closely. Her tolerance to coke was taking its toll, and it didn't make her energetic or happy anymore. She couldn't pinpoint for me how much she was using at this point but could only say "a lot." She started to believe she wasn't getting "good stuff" and was frustrated. She had been snorting heavily for about four months. She began calling in sick and wanted to stay in bed all day. She was acknowledging that she had a problem but believed it would stop. Her depression deepened, and her marriage was on the rocks.

After calling in sick two days in a row, staying in bed, and getting up only to snort a line, Nicole began to hit bottom. The cocaine was doing nothing for her but making her feel guilty for lying to everyone. She had to tell someone, and so she called her aunt, who she knew would not react negatively and would not judge. Her aunt listened and basically helped Nicole come to the conclusion that she was a cocaine addict. Nicole called her counselor and got right in. She confessed everything to her counselor, who said that inpatient rehab might be in order. Nicole now realized she was addicted but wasn't too sure about an inpatient program. She fought it for two hours.

Nicole finally called Renee to ask her to come to the counselor's office and allowed the counselor to tell her what was happening. Renee was actually relieved because she had been thinking it was much worse. As a good friend, she encouraged Nicole to go into treatment. Renee and Nicole drove there after leaving the counselor's office. Nicole deleted the drug dealer's number from her phone and cried the entire way, feeling sure her husband would divorce her.

Nicole called her mom and husband while she was waiting to be admitted. Her mom was relieved; her husband was in shock. "I couldn't talk to either of them that night. I felt too ashamed," she says.

No one ever knows what to expect in a treatment facility. They never think that the people will be friendly and welcoming, but they are. All Nicole wanted was to be alone and quiet. One night she was in her room, and there was an announcement for all patients to report for the 12-Step meeting for alcoholics. Nicole didn't budge. Someone knocked on her door and told her she had to go. "I'm not an alcoholic; I don't need to go," was her response. The person at the door laughed and went on. The nurse came in and told Nicole she had to go to all meetings. She went.

Nicole's first full day in rehab was a Saturday, and her husband came to visit. He brought her a notebook and a pen, telling her he thought she might be able to use them. He confessed he didn't have a clue as to what had been going on. He felt betrayed and disappointed. Nicole told him she wasn't half as bad as some of the other people in treatment. It wasn't funny.

She started writing in the notebook the next day. It became a part of her. She described feeling numb and how she couldn't cry anymore. She was worried about what people would think about her but began feeling a bit more comfortable there with other addicts.

By day three, she was feeling stronger. She was able to call her manager at work and her dad. They supported her immediately. She was not criticized and was reassured that all would be okay. Nicole was amazed that people were proud of her for what she was doing. Her counselor was encouraging her to report herself to the Board of Nursing—a consequence she wasn't quite ready to face. Nicole felt anxious and restless but on the sixth day wrote this quote on the top of a page of her notebook: "If you think in your heart, so shall you be." This gave her the confidence to call the board. Her license was suspended. When Nicole left the treatment facility, she made the decision to go to intensive outpatient (IOP) treatment. At one week sober, she was crying all day and a big ball of emotions. She later discovered this was okay, and she learned to take it one day at a time.

In the IOP program, Nicole was able to focus on her depression, anxiety, and addictions. She dove into 12-Step meetings headfirst. Things at home were quiet, but she hadn't talked to her husband about everything. So it wasn't long before Nicole was feeling frustrated and depressed again and struggling with her marriage, her toddler, and her husband's lack of support.

Nicole relapsed on cocaine. She acted as if she were going to IOP but instead met up with two other people with whom she had been in rehab. They bought beer, cocaine, and did it up all night. Her family was calling her cell phone all night, and Nicole was ignoring it. After hours of being drunk and high, she called Renee.

She wouldn't tell her where she was but only that she had relapsed. Renee met up with her the following day and sat with Nicole and let her cry it out again.

She allowed Renee to call her husband, who had been talking with the IOP counselor. Renee drove her to the hospital, where she was admitted to the psych unit. Nicole was so angry that she manipulated the doctor into discharging her the next day. Her husband, though, had read her journal and Nicole's statements about suicide and put her right back in. It took five days for Nicole to calm down and talk.

A family meeting was set up. She said it felt like an intervention. It was! Her husband, mom, stepdad, dad, sister-in-law, counselor, and Renee were there. Nicole felt as if they were ganging up on her. They had all decided that she wasn't going to return to home when she was discharged. She would move temporarily into her mom's house to concentrate on herself and hopefully avoid the daily frustrations.

Nicole spent eight days in the psych unit and then went to live with her mom. She got back into meetings and got a sponsor. She went back to IOP. She was not working, so she had all day, every day to work on recovery. She was back on track. She was trying to be a good mother to her son.

Her husband, though, seemed to be drinking more while living alone. Occasionally, Nicole would go home to visit with her son, and her husband would go out and not come back. The holidays were terrible. Right before Christmas, the couple talked, and he told Nicole he wasn't sure what he wanted. Nicole got overly emotional and went back to her mom's and took all seven of the sleeping pills she had left in a bottle. It was a weak attempt to kill herself, but she just wanted all the bad feelings to go away.

Once again, Nicole ended up in the ER and stayed overnight. Then she got back on the road to sobriety.

After the holidays, her husband asked for a divorce. Nicole could measure her growth by the fact that instead of relapsing at this news, she ran to a meeting to find her sponsor. She said, "I was a complete mess, but a sober mess."

She begged him to reconsider. He couldn't. Nicole could only dedicate her life to the recovery process: recovery from drugs, alcohol, depression, and now divorce ... you name it!

"I have come to realize that God has me right where He wants me to be. There was a reason for this rough course in my life, and He is revealing it to me little by little."

Her divorce was finalized when she was seven months sober. Today, Nicole says, "I have come to realize that God has me right where He wants me to be. There was a reason for this rough course in my life, and He is revealing it to me little by little. I am living life one day at a time and being the best mom that I can be. I am blessed."

Kelly

Your pain is the breaking of the shell that encloses your understanding.

—Khalil Gibran

One of the most difficult, heart-wrenching situations is to know your child, your baby, is an addict. There are few parents who will believe this to be true of their son or daughter without a great deal of proof. Denial is a strong reaction to overcome, but when the facts become obvious, what do you do? Where do you go for help? The answers are not always clear.

Kelly is a divorced mom. Her only child, Johnny, is a recovering drug addict. Kelly had been married to Johnny's dad for only two years before they divorced, so as a young child, Johnny saw his dad only on occasion.

Kelly worked part-time, and Johnny, like most kids today who have working moms, spent time with the babysitter but not every day. Both Johnny's dad and Kelly had a number of siblings who lived close by, and Johnny was the firstborn on both sides. He was never unloved or ignored. Johnny grew up in a very loving home and was the center of attention. Being a single mom, Kelly spent a great deal of time with her son and never once thought she wasn't a good parent.

Kelly describes Johnny as a happy, carefree child. He was also a risk taker like both of his parents. He was social but, as one of those sensitive little boys who wear their hearts on their sleeves, seemed to have a difficult time fitting into his parochial school crowd.

When Johnny was about thirteen, his personality began to change. He started to get moody. Within the next two years, he had changed his group of friends and began dressing in dark colors, and his moodiness got worse. He was also becoming a very talented drummer, and so his parents thought perhaps these changes just came with the territory. Teenagers do make changes, but most of these are short-lived. There was no reason to believe there were any real problems except for the tremendous amount of conflict and turmoil between Johnny and his dad. It seems his dad was not only extremely controlling but also emotionally abusive to both him and Kelly.

Other people began to comment on Johnny's behavior. At first Kelly said she felt bad and ashamed and didn't want anyone to know about her family issues. Still, she is an open person and knew she had to talk about it. Kelly began emailing Johnny's teachers and reached out to everyone in her family as well as her coworkers (at the time she was an RN in the ER). Her friends were the ones who said he was probably smoking pot, but Kelly's reaction was "no way!"

Kelly had a heart/head struggle but made the tough decision to screen Johnny for drugs. He was fourteen and tested positive for marijuana. Kelly reacted as any parent would: She was devastated.

Kelly felt horrible that he was even trying drugs but didn't think that it could be an addiction. A lot of kids experiment but then realize it isn't going to work for them. They stop before it gets serious and even before their parents can suspect them. But being a single mom, Kelly couldn't stop wondering what she had done wrong. She had spent so much time with him when he was a child. She felt that she had done everything a good mom possibly could do. "The most heartbreaking, devastating thing you will ever go through with your child is to know they feel so bad or sad about themselves that they do not respect themselves," Kelly tells me.

> *"The most heartbreaking, devastating thing you will ever go through with your child is to know they feel so bad or sad about themselves that they do not respect themselves."*

Johnny's drug use escalated. He was running away and not coming home for three to four days at a time. Kelly had to trap him at school and call crisis intervention. She knew if she brought him home, he would run again. The worst was when Kelly and her mom showed up at school to find Johnny, being held by the police, yelling that he would kill her if she took him back home. Kelly felt she had no choice but to place him in a local drug-rehab facility. He was there four days. What Kelly didn't know was that Johnny's dad was conspiring with their son to have Johnny live full-time with him—because Kelly must be crazy with all of this drug stuff, and he had to save Johnny! Johnny was a bit over fifteen, and he didn't like Kelly's rules anyway. She had tried drug screening and made him face the consequences of his actions. His dad, on the other hand, let him do whatever he wanted. What almost-sixteen-year-old, doing drugs, would not have opted to live with Dad?

For about a year and a half, Kelly did not see much of Johnny. Then one day while she was at work, she got a phone call from her son, saying he needed to get to the hospital immediately. His dad was with him. Kelly left work to meet them, and when she saw him, she knew she had to get him to the closest emergency room. She was scared and in shock. Johnny couldn't breathe, and what Kelly remembers is screaming "my son needs help now!" Kelly stayed in the hospital by his bedside for two nights. Her prayers were that his father would see the light and would take this seriously and help. Up to that point, he had been just looking the other way. He told Kelly that prior to this overdose, Johnny had come home beat up and said someone had put a gun to his head.

The whole time Johnny was in the hospital, his father could only talk about where to "put him." Kelly tells me that one of her memories of this period was seeing her son so sick and just holding him close to her. She would help him to the bathroom, and he would put his arms around her and say "I love you, Mom." She would rub his back. Although devastated, Kelly holds these precious memories as a blessing.

Johnny continued to live with his dad, but Kelly tried to stay involved and do the best she could even at a distance. She felt alienated from both Johnny and his dad. She fought for him through the courts, by hiring a lawyer, trying to have Johnny's hair follicles tested again, and trying to get him at least outpatient treatment (his dad still would not even consider inpatient). She was consistently disappointed. Kelly also knew she needed to seek advice from a professional. It was very frustrating because people wanted to help but didn't know what to do, and Kelly didn't either. She thought she was doing everything she possibly could.

Little by little, Johnny started coming around and asking Kelly for things. She started taking him shopping for clothes or out to dinner. Once in a while she gave him money. She did not believe she was enabling him; his dad was able to do that just fine all by himself.

What Kelly didn't know at that time was that Johnny was now into heroin. Marijuana had lived up to its name as a "gateway drug." He was smoking black tar heroin. When Kelly found out, she hit *her* bottom! Prior to this, she had been hoping and praying that Johnny would not have to face a bottom that would be devastating. She had wanted to hold an intervention with Johnny, but her ex-husband would not have any part of it. He insisted that Johnny was really fine and that he could handle him. Of course, Johnny had only gotten worse.

Kelly called a friend and got the name of a Ph.D. who came highly recommended for this type of situation. If Johnny couldn't get well, then she would have to get well herself. It was the only way she would be able to survive.

The doctor was expensive, but Kelly didn't care. She was a mess. It was Kelly's time, and unbeknownst to her, the intervention was going to be for her. The doctor felt that in order for her to be strong enough to even consider an intervention for Johnny, she had to be stable enough to learn not to enable her son. It was suggested that she go into rehab—because it truly was her choice. The doctor felt that time was of the essence and a rehab facility would be able to do in one week what it would take Kelly six months to do herself. Kelly knew it would help her to see what part she was playing in her son's disease and how his disease had affected her.

Time was of the essence, and a rehab facility would be able to do in one week what it would take Kelly six months to do herself.

She called work that day and asked for the following week off. Once she got into the program, she realized that she was the only one without a family member participating or there as an inpatient. It didn't matter. All Kelly knew was that she was going insane and could no longer help her son.

In that week, Kelly learned many things. With the help of the doctor she had first seen and treatment, she found out that she had to let Johnny figure it out for himself; that she had to make it hard enough for him; that it was okay to not like where he was but to let him know she loved him and was ready to help him when *he* was ready to be healthy again. She would not be a part of the problem any longer but would keep reminding him that he was a special young man. Kelly texted Johnny often and told him how much she loved him. She had come a long way. Before treatment Kelly's sleep was mostly filled with nightmares of Johnny overdosing and her performing CPR. Her thoughts now were focused on God's plan for him and her love for him. If Kelly had to continue to be the "bad person" to Johnny and his dad, that was going to be okay. All she wanted was her child alive.

If Kelly had to continue to be the "bad person" to Johnny and his dad, that was going to be okay. All she wanted was her child alive.

Miracles happen. They really do. Kelly was about five months out of her own rehab, working a 12-Step program and getting stronger every day. The day before his nineteenth birthday, Johnny called. He told her he had been clean of heroin for twenty-one days. He had hit his bottom, and although Kelly was sick to her stomach to hear that he had been shooting up, she felt hope. It is all about hope! Johnny then did something "heroic," as Kelly called it. He went to detox for four days, started working the steps, and got a sponsor. He called two of his friends (drug buddies) and told them he couldn't hang with them anymore. He went home and cried like he had never cried before. He went with Kelly to her doctor, and together they came up with a contract he had to follow if he wanted Kelly's help, with help being for rent, gas, food, and any other essentials.

Johnny got sober. Kelly realizes that he has to work his own program and she has to work hers. It isn't easy, because no matter the situation, a parent still wants to think she knows best. Kelly doesn't always agree with Johnny. He is supposed to be seeing the counselor, but he isn't. He has a full-time job and a girlfriend who Kelly believes is a good influence on him. Kelly does not believe Johnny is still working a step program. Today Kelly knows that it isn't about her and, that no matter what, she will be there if he needs her and can respect her. She feels he needs a lot more support in the long term to maintain his sobriety.

Her hope for Johnny is that he can find his true self, happiness, and self-esteem and realize what a wonderful, unique human being he is. She wants him to know he can do amazing things with and in his life, and she wants him to live fully. Johnny's plans today are to go to school and study psychology and work as an addiction specialist. He has asked the doctor to help him with this career path. Oh, and by the way, Johnny never gave up the drums. He has become an incredible drummer and has spent time playing in a band.

What about Kelly today? Kelly admits that she has had some slipups with Johnny, giving him money here and there. But Kelly's strengths far outnumber her relapses. Kelly works a 12-Step program, regularly goes to meetings, continues to see the psychologist when she feels she needs to, and prays—a lot! She believes that God is the only answer and that she never gave up on her deep faith in God. She calls the psychologist her "guardian angel" and believes that her life today is the culmination of many, many miracles.

You have to learn how to separate the person from the disease.

If you have an addicted son or daughter or think you might, please heed Kelly's advice. "You have got to reach out and support number one! You have got to take care of yourself and show that you care and will do anything for your child as long as they are helping themselves. Be a part of the solution not the problem. You have to have some type of faith; you cannot get over these tragedies without it. Each child is different, but I think they have to want to do it bad enough for themselves and hit their own bottom. Go to 12-Step meetings. Really get into a program. They help so much. And always, if it is possible, be united with your spouse. Be on the same page with discipline. You cannot do this on your own. You do not have the capability, because you love this person so much you are blinded and hurt for them. This is where codependency comes in to play. You have to learn how to separate the person from the disease. And *never, ever* give up on your child!"

Lindsey

> But He said to me, "My grace is sufficient for you, for my power is made perfect in weakness." Therefore I will boast all the more gladly about my weaknesses, so that Christ's power may rest on me.
> —2 Corinthians 12:9

Lindsey is twenty-six, single, and an educated young woman living on the West Coast. If you ask her what she is addicted to, she will say "anything and everything." The truth is Lindsey is an alcoholic, a drug addict, and suffers from bulimia.

Like many addicts, she is the child of an alcoholic mother who never entered recovery by her own choice. When Lindsey was a child, she never knew what she would wake up to and remembers often falling asleep to the sound of her mother screaming and fighting with her father and her older brother.

That she was twelve when she decided to drink and smoke pot seems so very young. But if you lived in the type of household she did, you'd want to escape, too. She also began to suffer from an eating disorder at the time and today says it was "anorexia masked by drugs."

Lindsey was searching for something but wasn't even sure what it was. She wanted to shed the Ugly Duckling image she had of herself, and, like most addicts, she already felt she was not good enough for her parents and was generally uncomfortable with life as she knew it. She consciously changed friends and started defying authority. She sought out the coolest kids she could find and worked to fit right in with the group. She would do anything to be cool, and that meant drinking, smoking cigarettes, and smoking pot with her new friends. Lindsey loved the feeling of being totally out of her mind—stoned or drunk—it didn't matter. It just felt good not to be her.

Lindsey loved the feeling of being totally out of her mind—stoned or drunk—it didn't matter. It just felt good not to be her.

Lindsey was a "blackout drinker" but still called it fun. It masked all her insecurities and gave her the self-esteem she felt she actually didn't possess. She had a super sense of ego when she was high and loved every second of that.

Lindsey was now a freshman in high school. Her friends were the same, but the fact that they were juniors upped her bravado further. She tried speed when they did, and because she liked it so much, she did it every chance she could. Cocaine was next. I mean, why not? She liked that even more. Still, there were a couple of drugs she wasn't as crazy about—acid and mushrooms. Why do you think she didn't care for them? Because she didn't feel she could drink when she took these and didn't feel in control!

By the end of her freshman year, Lindsey says she was doing it all and spent the summer in complete oblivion. Smoking, drinking, drugging, promiscuity, lying, cheating: You name it; she was into it and did it with purpose. The purpose was to get blitzed and "chill." She was successful in her efforts.

Sophomore year in high school was a repeat of her first year, but her junior year brought Ecstasy and pills. She continued to stick to her usual diet of speed, coke, and alcohol. Lindsey did not recognize her eating disorder (still likely anorexia) but thrived on people's comments about how tiny she was. She was being noticed, a positive thing for her, but admits she never got to the point of being so thin she couldn't play soccer or that anyone expressed concern over her weight. On the other hand, as with her addictions, she was attentive and manipulative enough to stay just under the radar of anyone who might get in the way.

Senior year was a quieter time in Lindsey's life, not because she chose it, but because all the friends she partied with had graduated and, for the most part, left town. The kids her age didn't party the way she did. Her older sister also had warned her that if she didn't get good grades, she would never be able to get out of her hometown and away from her parents. This did not mean full sobriety, but it did mean that she had to focus on school enough to get done, out, and on to college.

Ah, college! Away from home and a freshman year spent blacking out Thursday night through Sunday morning. She did some drugs, although her college friends did not. But they thought drinking was the most incredible thing they could do. Lindsey knew there were better highs, but since she had company drinking, well, drinking it would be and always to the extreme!

You've heard of the "freshman fifteen"? Remember how thin Lindsey had been in high school? Before her sophomore year, the pounds came off quickly because complications after she had her wisdom teeth removed prevented her from eating normally for approximately two months. When she got back to school, the thought of all that weight terrified her. Stopping the alcohol was not an option, and so in order to maintain her weight, she began purging. Why not? Throwing up seemed a very easy, completely rational way to keep from gaining back the weight.

It is hard to believe that life could get worse for Lindsey, but it did. In her mind, though, it got better in some respects. She had a very serious car accident (the bad) but ended up taking Vicodin and Soma for the majority of the summer (the good). She came up with a fantastic cocktail of one Vicodin plus two Somas with a side of four to six glasses of wine, vodka, or whatever drink was available. The accident changed nothing but the level of her addiction.

Lindsey says she "cleaned up" a bit in her senior year because she was living with her sister, brother-in-law, and their two small children. Between this change in environment and a very demanding college program, she didn't have as much time to party. She wanted to graduate and graduate on time.

And she did. Lindsey moved after that to work for a woman she describes as "beautiful, rich, successful, magnetic, and a raging alcoholic." The beauty of their relationship was that she drank as much as Lindsey drank but paid for it all. Bliss was then finding out that a cocaine dealer lived next door.

Lindsey was twenty-two years old, making more money than she knew how to spend, with a dream job, the thinnest she had ever been, and living in an area of the country that has been described as Eden. At this time Lindsey attributed her "thinness" to the fact that her job was stressful and her boss didn't eat. When she began to eat normally, she gained weight.

Lindsey clearly remembers her bottom. "I was in denial but definitely realized I couldn't stop my self-destructive ways. I became desperate to fill the gaping hole that was sure to consume me at any moment." It is hard to believe her drinking could get worse, but it did. It wasn't even important any longer to drink with people she knew, and she began waking up or coming to after a blackout with strange men. This started happening more and more frequently. She talked about hating herself, her life, and what she was doing but had no idea how to stop. This culminated in a nervous breakdown of sorts, and she decided to go to a 12-Step meeting. Oddly enough, she did not go to a meeting for recovering addicts but to one for family/ friends of addicts. Why? Denial. Lindsey knew she needed something but was not convinced she was the problem. She admits today that it took a major perspective shift to finally acknowledge she was an alcoholic and an addict. Her problems were the fault of everyone else, and she honestly saw herself as just a binge drinker. Her cocaine use had more of a grip on her than alcohol did, but she believed getting free was just a matter of willpower.

While she was in total denial about her alcohol and drug addiction, she recognized the truth about her bulimia. Actually, this problem was worse. She was unbelievably embarrassed, was too ashamed to tell anyone, and didn't know how to stop.

After attending a few 12-Step meetings for nonaddicts, she finally figured out she was not only an alcoholic, but also a drug addict with an eating disorder. She made a decision to go to 12-Step meetings for both her alcohol/drug addictions as well as her eating.

Lindsey did have someone very important in her life to share her efforts toward recovery. Her sister went into rehab for a Vicodin addiction and would subsequently bring Lindsey to meetings with her.

Once Lindsey made the decision to stop drinking, it wasn't easy. She admits to a few slips in early recovery. She smoked pot, took a Vicodin with "intent," and did a "whip-it" out of a whipped-cream can...twice! Her drug use and bulimia were already fully intertwined before she started working on recovery. Once she stopped drinking and drugging, the bulimia got totally out of control, and she couldn't go a day with-

She was unbelievably embarrassed, was too ashamed to tell anyone, and didn't know how to stop.

out purging. Abstinence from bulimia is technically not throwing up, and although she was working a program, she relapsed within the first thirty days. Lindsey says that "food is way more challenging for me than drugs and alcohol. I can deal with just not picking up a drink or a drug, but at some point I have to eat, and it is usually a slippery slope. To this day it is still a struggle, but by the grace of God, I haven't thrown up in two years!"

I ask Lindsey if through all those years, anyone had seen her addictions, and if so, did they say anything to her? Her response is that no one ever mentioned any-thing back then. No one knew about her bulimia until she told them. Once she opened up, she found out that there was some concern about her odd eating behaviors and drastic measures to lose weight. Like all good addicts, though, Lindsey says she did "quite a good job at fooling everyone into believing I was okay. I was handling life great. My outsides looked in order. No one knew the hell I was truly in." When she made amends to an old friend, his response was "Wow, Linds. You were really good at hiding all of this." She realizes how good she had been at lying, deceiving, and manipulating. "I almost began to believe myself!"

"My outsides looked in order. No one knew the hell I was truly in."

Today Lindsey attends 12-Step recovery meetings for both alcohol/drugs and bulimia on a regular basis. She works with a sponsor. She continues to maintain her sobriety by being of service, talks to her sponsor and/or someone in the program at least once a day, and works with sponsees.

If Lindsey were to give advice to others about how she feels the addict in someone's life should be treated, she would say "Love them. Support them. Give them space and ask how you can help. I think the most frustrating part about telling people about my addictions and eating disorder is their reaction, especially to my bulimia. I don't want people to be watching my every move and to be commenting on what I'm eating or not eating or about my weight. Many of these reactions tend to be extremely triggering for me. So just ask the person how you can be supportive and not overbearing or completely detached."

Matt

Secrecy, once accepted, becomes an addiction.

—Edward Teller

If you are not sure exactly what a sex addict is, or the type of behavior that might characterize one, I hope you will have a much better understanding after reading this story. The sex addict is your friendliest neighbor, supermom or dad, or your best friend at work. They live very secret lives. They live double lives. They seldom harm anyone but themselves and, of course, the family that loves them.

This is a story told to me by Matt. Matt is a fifty-two-year-old sex addict whom I had the pleasure of getting to know on a drive to a residential treatment center where he is a regular speaker. He tells his story without shame or blame, which is something that has taken him a number of years to do. His story isn't only about his addiction but his relationships as well.

Matt grew up in the Midwest and was the son of an alcoholic and pill-addicted mother. His father was his absolute best friend but enabled his mother's behaviors for as long as Matt could remember. Growing up he didn't realize that his mother was an alcoholic. She had mood swings, and she could get angry, so you were supposed to stay away from her when she acted that way. Because of her drinking (she also smoked about four to five packs of cigarettes a day), his mom was verbally abusive. It made Matt feel "less than," words he didn't understand until he went into recovery.

He admits he was one angry kid. Who wouldn't be if he was cut with a knife, burned with a cigarette, stuck with a carving fork, and hit with a belt from time to time by his mother? Dad, as the peacekeeper, never addressed Mom's behavior but just kind of made it all go away. Yes, Matt was angry. But when you are made to feel less than and feel shame, then anger is about the best tool available to combat those emotions.

Matt has an older sister, but she wasn't really much help to him as a compassionate sibling. She rebelled at a very early age. She was smoking cigarettes in sixth grade. Before long, she was smoking marijuana. She finished high school but never college. She is fifty-five years old and has never held a job. She is a heroin addict who lost both a husband and a fiancé to drugs. Matt hasn't seen her in years. When their mom died, Matt deposited a large sum of money into a bank in trust for his sister. It should have lasted her whole life. It is almost gone. Matt understands enabling and has already made the decision that if she comes to him for money, the answer will be an emphatic "No!"

Anger wasn't Matt's only problem. He was full of resentments, but what becomes important is that he had no respect for women. He tells me he dated a bit in high school and in college. In his post-college years, though, he dated a lot and isn't sure it would be considered "healthy dating." Speed dating was more like it. He understands today that it was impossible for him to respect women because he didn't even respect himself. He didn't like who he was; he describes himself as "obnoxious, angry, full of myself, and at the same time very low self-esteem, but I just never knew it."

Matt married. He dated his wife (now ex-wife) for about a year and a half before they took the plunge. He tells me that he knew he would marry her the minute he met her and that he has strong feelings for her to this day. But they found out that they both brought serious issues into the marriage that were never addressed. They actually were quite alike. They both had rather low self-esteem and a fear of intimacy. They also had a lot of interests in common and a great deal of fun as a young married couple.

"You can drift in a marriage for ten, fifteen, twenty years and not even know it until one day you wake up and you are a stranger in your own home with the person you are living with," Matt says. This relates to his compulsive sexual behavior, which started innocently enough, as most all addictive behaviors do.

"You can drift in a marriage for ten, fifteen, twenty years and not even know it until one day you wake up and you are a stranger in your own home with the person you are living with."

Matt says he was not an Internet guy. As a matter of fact, when his behaviors emerged, the Internet didn't even exist. He was never an image guy. He dallied with phone sex for a few years on and off but says that was more of an introduction. He was never interested in same-sex or underage kids (he truly is grateful that these were not part of his addiction). It started when he would take business trips. He would be out on the road and seek out a massage parlor or have a masseuse come see him in his room. At first it was just nonintercourse sex acts. Most of us have heard of a "happy ending" in these situations, and Matt says they went on for years and years and years. It was easy to justify these, he feels, because in his mind it wasn't really having sex, and who was he hurting anyway? He "graduated" to occasional intercourse but only on the road because, once again, that could be justified.

The behaviors became unmanageable. He couldn't control the feelings. He couldn't control the compulsion. He didn't "act out" daily but certainly a couple of times a week. But it occupied his thoughts in an unhealthy, compulsive way. What Matt describes to me as the hard part was the secret life, the double life, the lies, and the manipulation. "When it comes out of your mouth, you believe what you are saying after a while and having to manage that double life at the same time when you go to 'medicate.' My drug of choice was a hooker or a massage therapist, and you feel worse than before, so the shame and the guilt became overwhelming."

Sex addicts have bottoms like any other addict. And, like any other addict, many are completely ignored for any number of reasons. Matt describes bottoms that should have led him directly into therapy, but didn't quite do it: He was held up at gunpoint. That wasn't enough to quit. He got caught up in a sting operation. He walked into a hotel room and was cuffed and stuffed (as he puts it). He spent the night in jail. Then he had to go before a judge but was let go on his own recognizance. It was a misdemeanor (solicitation). He was on the road at the time, so no one had to know about it, not even his wife.

Matt says he could make all sorts of excuses for his behaviors, but part of the reason he could not address his compulsion was because he never recognized it as an addiction and thought he could stop when he wanted to. Denial. What addicted person hasn't been there? The closest Matt came to getting help was after he was involved in a road-rage incident. This was unrelated to his sexual activities but certainly tied in to his anger. Matt recognized his anger issues after this incident and went to see a therapist, but there was no discussion that even got remotely close to his sexual addiction. Matt feels today that the therapist just didn't know to go there, and he didn't either. His secret life was still with him, and there were so many reasons to stop, but he just wasn't ready.

He and the family (his wife and two children at this point) had moved to the Northeast for what Matt describes as that "job that if it sounds too good to be true, it is," and they were all miserable. So they came to the conclusion that they would move to the Southwest. It would be a fresh start and also the geographic shift that most all addicts do at least once in their addiction. Surprisingly, things got better. He and his wife were having sex for the first time in quite a while. He says it wasn't frequent but there was actually a bond and a feeling of intimacy that hadn't been there in a long time. During that time, his wife began having pain during intercourse, and as a result, the sex ceased. They lived in the same house but without intimacy. They never talked about it, never addressed it. They learned to live that way and accept that as normal. The important thing, as Matt continuously reiterates, is that "it is not about the sex; it is about the intimacy."

Whether or not his lack of intimacy at home was the catalyst, Matt's activities started to escalate. He spent more and more time and money in massage parlors and with prostitutes and was obsessing about this in every waking moment. In his words, "I raised my hand and said, 'I can't do this anymore. I can't manage my secret life anymore. I can't manage the lies, the deception anymore.' And I went to see a therapist." He told his wife he wanted to seek treatment because he had "some issues he felt he needed to sort out." It took him two months to get up the courage to actually make an appointment.

Matt likens a good therapist to a good pair of shoes: You have to keep going until you find the ones that fit. He was fortunate because he found that "fit" immediately. The therapist agreed that Matt suffered from a sexual compulsion, and they went to work with the intent of having a disclosure with his wife when they were ready. (A "disclosure" is a detailed account of the sex addict's acting-out behavior. It is all-inclusive and gives an overview of the things the addict has done throughout his or her life. It is recommended a therapist always be present.) The therapist also suggested that Matt go to a 12-Step meeting for sex addicts. He honestly wasn't sure since his impression of such meetings was of a group of people holding hands, singing "Kumbaya," drinking Kool-Aid, and talking about God. He didn't think that this sort of thing was for him, and after all, he was stopping without anyone's help.

The therapist taught Matt how to describe his feelings. He didn't even know he had feelings. He found it difficult and probably a waste of time, but he did it anyway. He learned for the first time in his life how to honestly express himself. He went to a meeting and thought it was great, but in his mind he was still thinking "I'll go to therapy, a few meetings, and be done." When the therapist asked him when he would be going to his next meeting, he was a bit startled. It got worse when she asked him how many meetings he thought he would get to the following week! Matt says, "I didn't know what the hell she was talking about. Then she started talking to me about a sponsor."

> The therapist taught Matt how to describe his feelings. He didn't even know he had feelings.

Matt went to another meeting and identified the guy he thought could be his sponsor. When he told his therapist he had found someone, she described him perfectly. She had never met the man. Matt says, "This was my first of many God moments. I don't believe in coincidences anymore." The gentlemen did become his sponsor and today is a close, personal friend.

I ask Matt if his wife had any idea that he was going to the meetings and what they were for. He says that she knew he was going to a group, but he told her it was with people who sit around and talk about their feelings. Because she knew he was seeing the therapist, that wasn't exactly a red flag. But Matt knew he was headed toward disclosure. With the help of his therapist, he had written a couple of drafts, six pages long, detailing his behaviors, feelings, and thoughts.

One afternoon when his wife came home from bowling, she sat Matt down and said, "There are so many girls that are getting divorced at bowling, and their relationships are all screwed up, and I want to know if I'm going to spend the rest of my life with you. I want to know who I'm married to. Something's not right, but I can't put my finger on it. You can tell me. It's okay." Matt had a choice: He could either tell her one more lie, or he could tell her the truth. He chose the truth.

As Matt puts it, "It got, as you can imagine, really ugly." He told her what had been going on and today realizes that it was a big mistake, not the information, but the timing. "I would never recommend to anybody making a disclosure without a therapist present." They did have the formal disclosure with the therapist, but promptly after that, the therapist closed her office due to a personal crisis. So Matt's wife had all this information about her husband of twenty-plus years literally dumped on her and could talk to no one. As for Matt, well, he had already unloaded and was feeling better. He was going to meetings, had a sponsor, had learned to journal, meditate, and do all the things he knew he had to do, but his wife was just kind of "out there."

Things actually got better for a while. They were doing some weekly checks and feedback, but then something would happen at home, and she would choose to take the "dark side" as Matt calls it today. Instead of trying to make the relationship work, she would continue to ask him questions whose answers she already knew. She went to a place of mistrust, and to this day, Matt tells me, she doesn't trust him despite the number of amends and apologies he has made. At one point she went to a couple of codependency group meetings, but she never got well enough to lose even some of the anger.

Matt was in a very different place. He had learned through his program that it wasn't all about him. He was able to restore his self-esteem and live in the moment and with gratitude as opposed to worrying about what was or what will be.

Matt really wanted the marriage to work. Then one night, the couple went out to dinner, and she slid divorce papers across the table. She said she was done with the marriage and that she wanted to dissolve it in a public place because she was afraid of how he would react. She had also tried to get an order of protection against him even though there had never been any violence in their home. Instead of acting out of anger, Matt felt he responded with love and told her he loved her and always would and asked if she would take the weekend to reconsider. She was pretty blunt when she told him "I'm not reconsidering." Matt said he was sad but okay. They had been married for more than twenty-two years at that time, and for the last two years they had lived together, she had taken the bedroom, while he had had the "man cave." That "man cave" was a place of shame; it wasn't a healthy place to be.

A couple days later, she called looking for him. He had been at his attorney's office. She was surprised. He was confused. "You are filing for divorce, and I have my attorney," he told her. She thought about that and decided to rescind the papers at that point. She said, "I thought you would fight a little harder for me."

Matt felt he had done everything he could. "I begged you. I pleaded with you. I asked you to go to counseling. I asked you to do couples counseling. I asked you to work hard on working on you. And you rejected all of these things."

With all that said, there was still a glimmer of hope for them. They did a getaway to try to work through some issues. Matt says there was some yelling, scream-ing, and crying, but when it was all over, she invited him to sleep with her that night. It was completely nonsexual. She wanted to be held. They returned home feeling pretty good. The next night at home, Matt went to get in bed with her, and she said, "What are you doing? You are not welcome here!"

So that was the real beginning of the end. Within a few months she was raging at Matt in front of the kids. She said she would go to couples therapy if he had a session with the kids and admitted his behaviors. What she didn't know was that Matt, who had a very close relationship with both his son and daughter, had already talked to them close to a year before this. He believes his wife wanted the kids to feel sorry for her and think "what a total asshole Dad is." She honestly didn't believe the kids knew, so she forced the issue. At one point, Matt's son turned to his mom and said, "We know Dad has fucked up a lot, but we trust him. We don't trust you." That was devastating to her. It got worse. Matt's daughter looked at him and said, "Daddy, I forgave you a long time ago. I'll always love you."

Matt was still living at his home in the "man cave." Unfortunately, the children remained somewhat involved or at least had to witness to all the rage and anger. Matt's son finally said, "Mom, Dad has done everything you have asked him to for the last two years. Either forgive him or divorce him!" Very powerful! The next evening her decision was made. She said she was done, and Matt said okay. He moved out of the house.

Matt says it seemed like a role reversal. His wife was now in that dark, angry place where one lies and manipulates. "She had almost become the person I was," he tells me. Matt is not casting blame on his wife. Most assuredly, it takes two people to make a marriage work, and there were things he would have done differently. Facing his addiction, though, has made him strong. It has helped him regain his self-esteem. It has put him in touch with his feelings and how to express them. He is grateful for every day he has. Without the addiction, without recovery, he would still be living a lie. He would still be just one angry guy!

I talk to Matt about his ex-wife and what, exactly, she had wanted from him. He explains that a huge part of the problem was just her distrust and that he couldn't be intimate with her because she couldn't be intimate with him. She didn't want to work on issues together, and she didn't want to work on herself. She just wanted him to go back over every single detail of the years he acted out sexually.

This is when Matt drew a healthy boundary. Both his therapist and hers urged her not to go back. It seemed she now wanted to know every aspect of his addictive past, she wanted him to fix it, and she wanted it unrealistically, meaning *right now*.

Matt says he recognizes his shortcomings. He has addressed them and considers himself a work in progress. For the first time in his life, though, he has been able to have very healthy and intimate relationships with both men and women, specifically sharing his feelings with his friends in recovery. He does not condone his behavior, but he is no longer ashamed. He had also continued to send his ex-wife "olive branches" via email and text messages, asking if she would be willing to sit down and talk, to try to be friends. There was never a response. He tells me he ran into her the other day, and he got angry. Since he had been angry most of his life, he knows today that being angry is toxic to him.

Matt is not in a relationship at this time, but he is dating. He knows he is now capable of a healthy relationship with a woman. After two and a half years of sobriety and more than sixty sessions with a therapist, he is sure that he is beginning to figure out his life. He still checks in with a therapist every now and then for a "tune-up." He is not anxious to be involved in a relationship and believes it is all about timing. If the right person comes along, it will be the right time.

When Matt speaks to a group of addicts about his sex addiction, he ends the meeting by giving each one of them a small token: He gives them a small pocket guardian angel. Matt says that he is still in the early stages of a marathon called life. He is no longer just one angry man!

Tammy Jean

Religion is for those individuals trying to avoid going to hell. Spirituality is for those of us who have been there.

—United Methodist Church bulletin

Tammy Jean, age forty-five, tells me she just has an addictive personality. She is in recovery for her addiction to alcohol and prescription drugs. She is married and has two boys, ages twenty-three and sixteen. She chose to tell her story in a somewhat different format in response to specific questions. The message she sends is the same as the others: There is a solution and hope!

Do you have family members who suffer from any addictions? My mom and sister appear to have some food issues. My sister also might have an alcohol problem, but no one in my family would claim to have any addictions. My youngest son seems to use marijuana on a regular basis and is waiting for it to be legalized!

How old were you when you took your first drink/ drug? I think I was about eleven or twelve when I noticed my parents and their friends would leave drinks on the table. I went around the table and finished them all. I felt so grown up. I remember liking alcohol and wanting more.

How long were you in your disease before you got into recovery? I drank for more than thirty years. I started as a binge drinker at the age of fifteen, but eventually it became an everyday thing. I never made it more than a week without a drink in the early years. I was able to stop when I was pregnant with my two sons, and after they were born, I could control my drinking so I could get up with them at night. But I so looked forward to when I had a day off and an overnight sitter so I could drink as much as I wanted.

Did you believe you could stop if you wanted to? In the beginning, I never thought about it. I was still able to do everything I needed to do at home, work, and school, so not drinking didn't cross my mind. I actually scheduled when I partied and drank, and when it got too crazy, I would promise myself that I would get it back under control again. As time went on, everything began to revolve around when it would be time to drink again, whether the activity would involve drinking, and then before too long, forget the activity—let's drink!

One day I realized that I might not be able to stop, but I was unsure. Drinking was no longer fun but a necessity. My health was suffering, and I was in and out of doctors' offices and even hospitalized, but I never told them about my drinking. I wanted to get healthier, and so I wanted to eat better, take vitamins, read self-help books; I went to church and took prescriptions for everything. Some of these were for depression, anxiety, high blood pressure, insomnia, thyroid, and more! I worked

> "My health was suffering, and I was in and out of doctors' offices and even hospitalized, but never telling them about my drinking."

for a doctor who trusted me. I wrote my own prescriptions, she signed them, and then I would increase the dosage. I also went to other doctors, psychiatrists, and counselors to "balance" mind, body, and spirit. I knew myself better than anyone else, and I was definitely messed up.

The doctor I worked for suggested I take a break from all medications for a couple of days. I thought that made sense, but as a nurse, I also knew that no one should abruptly stop taking medications. The doctor didn't know that not only was I medicating, but I was also doing so with my own combination of meds and alcohol.

I didn't sleep for several days but thought that this was a good thing, that I was detoxing naturally. I was hoping my appetite would return also since I was rarely eating solid food. I had been in the habit of taking vitamins or liquid supplements to stay healthy because solid food didn't want to go down and stay down.

After not taking any of the medications, drinking, eating, or sleeping for several days, I had the first of my seizures. Since I had nothing in my system, the testing began. I never told the truth, and so they blamed these on stress. I had more seizures over a period of months. I convinced myself and everyone else that these were all due to genetics. I convinced myself that I would never feel good again, and that is when I began to think that I could quit when I wanted to, but why would I want to? I never felt good, nothing made me happy, and not drinking made it worse. I had lists of reasons why I should quit drinking because I was rational enough to know that I had to write notes to remember phone conversations and how bad the hangovers were, but I would just throw the lists away.

"I never felt good, nothing made me happy, and not drinking made it worse."

I look back today at that time and realize I rarely left the bedroom except to get and hide alcohol. My bedroom was my tomb to die in, and that is what I was waiting for. I wished to stop living because I didn't want to go to heaven and talk to God or be somewhere where there was no alcohol and no fun. Of course I also didn't want to go to a suffering hell, because if this wasn't hell already, what was hell? I didn't want to feel anything. I thought it would be a relief to all those around me if I was no longer alive. I had no purpose. I was just a burden.

Did others feel you drank too much (or thought you were an alcoholic) and did they tell you about it? I tried to stay away from people who didn't drink like me, or I tried to control my drinking around certain people and would go home and drink more. I remember a few times when someone would joke about how many drinks I must have had before I got to the party, but I blew it off. I figured they were jerks, and I would get my husband to say I was just fine. My parents never thought my drinking was a problem even when I was getting a divorce and moved in with them. I had been ordered out of my home by the court since I had lost custody of my uncontrollable teenager. My husband stayed in the home. There were piles of paperwork proving how unstable I was.

> "I remember a few times when someone would joke about how many drinks I must have had before I got to the party, but I blew it off."

Remember all those doctors I saw? Too bad I never told them the truth. I did behave irrationally at times, but they called it "stress." I would be fine if my husband just treated me better, if my children would behave, if my husband would make my children behave, and if I didn't have so much bad luck with work and health issues.

My husband kept hoping I could get over it and control my drinking and be happy. He finally stopped hoping and talking and began the separation/divorce process. He said he could no longer watch me destroy myself. That is when I moved in with my parents.

"I would be fine if my husband just treated me better, if my children would behave, if my husband would make my children behave, and if I didn't have so much bad luck with work and health issues."

Before I made the move, when my oldest son would come home from college and I tried to stay away from alcohol while he was home, I would be shaking and crying. He would try to take care of me and make me eat; he even fed me ice cream, and he would say things like "Mom, don't you want to see me graduate college and get married and play with your grandchildren?" My answer was no. I didn't see any happiness in any of that, and he would be better off if I were gone. Sometimes I would attempt a "nice" conversation with him, and if I could have had just the right amount of alcohol to do that, then I could be the mom I used to be. My youngest son, who had found my drugs, was living with my husband when I moved in with my parents. He didn't talk to me much at all, but when he did talk to me, it was usually something like "You don't remember, Mom, because you were probably drunk again."

How did all this make you feel? In the beginning, I ignored it. Then I became defensive, argumentative. I denied, lied, exaggerated, blamed, and became angry and tearful. Actually, I did whatever worked to get them off the topic of my drinking. As I headed toward the worst days, no one said anything anymore, and I didn't care about anything anyway except how I could get more to drink. I decided to drink, take a handful of Xanax, and pray for the end. I was exhausted and wanted to sleep and never wake up. But I did wake up, and I was in a hospital in the ICU, tied to a bed, with a sitter at my side. I yelled at the sitter, pulled out the tubes, and when the nurses came in and injected me with medication, I told them they couldn't hurt me anymore because I had already hurt myself. The

"As I headed toward the worst days, no one said anything anymore, and I didn't care about anything anyway except how I could get more to drink."

drugs immobilized me. My older son came in and saw me all tied up. I couldn't speak and had no expression on my face. He left the room quickly. All he could see were the tears coming down my face. He knew I was in there, in that shell of a body, and he knew that I was just so sad.

Was that your bottom? No. You would think so, but it wasn't. My bottom came during the final processing of the divorce. My oldest son didn't know what to say to me and was generally at college; my youngest son lived with my husband, and he never wanted to talk to me or see me again. He had issues with drugs and anger and at the time had a court-appointed attorney because no one could decide if he should be at home with his father or if the court would approve him to even visit my parents' home where I now stayed.

My physical health was at its worst. My hair was falling out in clumps, my face was withdrawn with dark circles under my eyes, and my blood pressure was through the roof. Doctors had warned me about stroke and heart attack possibilities. I couldn't tolerate food or even liquids at this point. Mentally, I was completely unstable: I had no sense of reality; I had no hope, joy, and absolutely no self-esteem. Any spirituality that I might have had at some point in my life was nonexistent. I was no longer working and knew with the way I looked no one would hire me. I wouldn't have gotten past the interview. I shook so bad I would be unable to shake anyone's hand, and most of all I couldn't stop drinking and drugging long enough to pass a drug test. I had been asked to leave my last job. They said I was too unhealthy and, after my extended leave of absence, decided we should part ways.

A family member called the police when I left the house—drinking and driving. I was arrested and jailed with a DUI, yet I went right back to drinking when I left jail. (This is another story in itself for another time.)

I was in the hospital again when a doctor came in and said, "Are you going to say what I want to hear so you can get out of here?" I replied, "Yeah. Pretty much." At least I was honest! It was Election Day, and he asked me who I was going to vote for because everyone was talking about change. I asked if I was getting out of the hospital so that I could vote. I didn't vote, but here is what happened to me: God must have heard the prayers of others because I no longer prayed. I thought about how that doctor said that I would say what I needed to as I had done so many times before. I thought, "God, I want this to be different this time." I didn't have a request for anything but change, and within me I heard God say, "It will be okay." That is all I heard, and yet, I felt different. It was not some kind of deal, like one of those "foxhole prayers." I felt a true

> "I thought, 'God, I want this to be different this time.'"

inner peace for the first time in my life, and as I tell you this, I start to cry because I know how close to death I had been so many times and had wanted to die so many times. And at that moment, I just knew it would be okay. I began to take baby steps of progress. I hadn't gotten out of the hospital to vote for a president, but I could vote for me—to begin taking care of me, figuring out me, finding me.

How about today? When I look back at my addiction, I suppose that I had many little interventions over the many years that were voices from others and even from within myself. I had put myself into therapy three times. I never did get admitted into an extended rehab through the many times when I was in the hospital. I was in psych units after ICU and detox. I know today that I could not surrender to God and seek recovery until I was ready and did it for myself. No matter how my children, spouse, and parents begged me to find a way to life, I just couldn't do it. That day in the hospital was my first true "spiritual awakening." I wanted to live, and I was going to figure out how to do that. I knew it could only be with God's help.

I have had a lot of support. Once my parents opened their eyes and accepted that I was not a victim to bad circumstances and saw me for who I was and had become, they could support me in a healthy manner. Even my husband (we did not divorce and are happily together now) supported me, although he was continuing the divorce process. My older son was an amazing source of support, and support continues to grow. As I change, others have reached out to me: friends, other family members, and now my younger son.

I work a 12-Step program, have a sponsor, and have more friends in the fellowship than I can even count. My marriage is the best it has ever been, I am close to my boys, and I now have not one but two great part-time nursing jobs. My physical health has been restored, and I find ways every day to live without alcohol and drugs.

Okay. Now I have to talk about relapse. I did have a slip about one and a half years after I made the decision to get sober. I could give a number of excuses, but none would be true. The reason I had a drink was this: I wanted to drink. I didn't want to be talked out of it. I thought maybe, just maybe, it would feel good, as it did so many years ago when it wasn't a problem. I planned it. I took the first sip, and you know what? It wasn't so good, so I drank a bit more. I realized what I was doing, and my head was full of 12-Step recovery stuff, everything I had overcome, and the "black" that had been deep inside of me returned.

I didn't finish the bottle. I called my sponsor, other women in the fellowship, and went to a meeting. I could have gotten away with it because no one knew. But God did, and I wanted to return to my vow to be honest, open, and willing (HOW). I knew if I didn't continue the recovery process, I would die. I chose sobriety for the second and what I hope is the last time in my life. I love slogans, and my own personal slogan is "AB": aware and beware. Stay aware of myself and what I need and maintain that regularly; beware of what I see as dangerous for me so that I can avoid it for the moment or for longer or set boundaries as I see when I need them.

What advice would you give someone who had to deal with an addict like yourself? Pray for them and give them support when they reach out to you. If it gets too exhausting for you to deal with, love them enough to let them go until they find their way. Never give up on them, and don't blame yourself for their poor choices or inability to recover.

Favorite phrase/slogan? Well, I mentioned my slogan of AB before, but there are a couple that I really love. One is "Destiny is not a matter of chance; it is a matter of choice," and the other is "Change your thinking, change your life." It works for me!

Last words? Yes. Thank you for allowing me to share!

Tracy

We are not creatures of circumstance; we are creators of circumstance.

—Benjamin Disraeli

Almost everyone has heard that alcoholism is a "family disease." Every type of addiction results in a "family disease." Some family members make a decision to get help for themselves regardless of whether their addicted loved one wants recovery or not. This is one of those stories and, like all the rest, has no ending... yet!

Tracy is forty years old and has three children, ages four, seven, and eleven. She has been married for fifteen years but is currently separated. Tracy is not an addict. Her father was a "functioning alcoholic," and she has a sister in recovery, but Tracy knew little about the disease because it was never discussed.

When troubles arise in any marriage, it is beneficial to call in that third party, the counselor, to help sort things out. So when Tracy and her husband were having problems, they made the decision to seek counseling. Tracy felt that she had completely shut down. She had put up a wall between herself and her husband, and she could not break it down. After a couple of questions from the counselor, she determined that she was holding on to strong resentments against her husband due to his binge drinking. It might seem obvious to others, but Tracy says she was "shocked to learn that the underlying cause of our troubles was related to my husband's alcoholism as well as my codependency."

On the advice of the counselor, Tracy's husband stopped drinking but felt he didn't need to get into a recovery program. Of course, he was in denial, and although Tracy was not herself in denial about her husband's disease, she continued to believe that their troubles would end. They didn't, because his erratic behavior didn't change, and Tracy found herself obsessing about his recovery and micromanaging everything he was doing. Addicts in recovery learn quickly that their addiction, whatever it might be, is a symptom. The real changes must be made in behaviors. In many cases, halting an addiction without a recovery support system only makes the addict angry and miserable, or angrier or more miserable. Tracy stayed miserable with her husband for another two months.

Tracy couldn't handle the idea that her husband was the one with the problem and yet she was the one going to meetings. She was furious.

The sister in recovery advised Tracy to go to a 12-Step meeting. The problem was that Tracy couldn't handle the idea that her husband was the one with the problem and yet she was the one going to meetings. She was furious. She attended the meetings and each time she heard "Keep coming back," so she did. At the meetings she would listen to what others had to say and began to identify with their stories. By recognizing the similarities little by little, she felt she was beginning to regain parts of herself that she had lost long ago within her codependent behaviors.

As time went on, Tracy was able to recognize the dysfunction in which she was living. Control was a big factor for her, and she had grown accustomed to controlling or wanting to control everything and everyone. Still while trying to control everything, Tracy became the victim of her own behavior and lost any real control over her own life.

Tracy's husband had gone without a drink for three years but was still not in a recovery program. Since he had stopped drinking without changing his behaviors, he would be what's considered a "dry drunk." Once Tracy understood her own role in the marriage, she realized how sick she had become as well. She began to see how she had ended up in such a relationship. She married someone she could take care of, someone she could control, and unfortunately, this was not the foundation for a good marriage and a healthy relationship. Tracy realized that she didn't love herself but hid that behind staying busy taking care of others.

Tracy had to change and in doing so had to admit her role in a marriage that was failing. Instead of trying to be the peacemaker, Tracy decided to just let the chaos happen and not be a part of it. Tracy had kept quiet for a long time to keep from arguing, but she had now learned to set boundaries and take care of herself. She also realized that she no longer could have someone in her life who did not want to get healthy.

She didn't discover any of this overnight. There were many counseling appointments, meetings, and a lot of prayer before she finally had the strength to ask her husband for a separation. To end her marriage after so long and with three children to consider was the most difficult thing she had ever had to do, but she realized that it would be more difficult to live with someone in total denial while still hoping for a perfect marriage.

Two days after Tracy filed for divorce, she took a three-week vacation with her children. Her husband attended his first 12-Step recovery meeting the evening before she left. One month before the divorce was finalized, he called Tracy asking if she would want to try to work things out. They met, and Tracy decided to give it one more try. After one week, Tracy realized he had not made any changes and that he didn't want sobriety enough to do whatever it takes. Tracy told him it was not going to work out.

Seven months after the initial filing, the divorce was granted. No one can make someone else get into recovery and be healthy, but Tracy prays that he will choose to do both for the sake of their children. Tracy will be just fine. She had been working on her own recovery program long before making the decision to end her marriage. Recovery takes time, and Tracy's life is moving forward. She has grown from this experience and credits the mercy, grace, and love of her Higher Power for her own recovery.

"The most important thing to know is that if you have an addict in your life, take a look at what your role is."

When someone is willing to share a recovery story with me, I always ask what advice that person would give someone who might be on that same path. Tracy says the most important thing to know is that if you have an addict in your life, take a look at what your role is. We become so enmeshed in the lives of others, especially those closest to us, that we lose sight of ourselves. Take the time to do the things that make you happy. Say the "Serenity Prayer" and let it speak to you. The gifts of peace and serenity are priceless.

Tracy recently updated her story for me. She has met an amazing man free of addiction. In her words, he is calm, emotionally available, and present, and she is now part of a loving, authentic relationship.

Rose

People have a hard time letting go of their suffering. Out of a fear of the unknown, they prefer suffering that is familiar.

—Thich Nhat Hanh

The one sure thing about addiction is that it isn't limited to any particular part of the world. Rose, a fifty-eight-year-old alcoholic in recovery, brings her story to us by way of England, Africa, and Canada. The life of an alcoholic is the same wherever you go, and the hope of recovery is equally as available. Rose is a late bloomer. She has been in recovery for five and a half years.

Rose would like to blame her drinking on her husband. But the reality is that she had a grandfather who was "maybe" an alcoholic, and today she realizes that her low self-esteem, lack of self-confidence, and need to be perfect as a child made her a prime candidate for the disease.

Born and educated in England, Rose got a Primary School Teacher diploma and decided to go teach in Kenya. After four years in the classroom, she was in the process of deciding whether to stay or not when she met her future husband. He was born and raised in Tanzania and had returned to "have some fun" before going back to England and his rocky seven-year marriage. He was spending time with his brother, and Rose was in awe of them both for their ability to party. Rose was drinking and smoking pot at that time but never to the extent that it affected her teaching.

Rose fell in love, and since he promised her the world, she gave up her position and followed him back to the United Kingdom. She knew after a few months of living with him (he had since separated from his wife) that he had woven a rather merry tale about how great life would be with him. Still, she loved him and thought he could do no wrong. Rose gave up ties to her family when they expressed concern; she didn't want that "aggravation." Rose was totally at his beck and call, and nothing else mattered. She sold what little she had so that they could have money for drinking.

The couple spent the next two years in a small flat in southern England. They enjoyed drinking but not to excess; on the other hand, any money they had went to alcohol before anything else. His divorce finally went through, and he and Rose married. It wasn't exactly the wedding of the year. The witnesses were people on the street they didn't even know, and there were no family members included. They had completely isolated themselves, and Rose was five months pregnant. This pregnancy ended in abortion and a serious attempt at suicide. A while later, Rose and her husband did the classic geographic shift: They moved to Canada.

With Rose pregnant once again, she and her husband made their home in Toronto. Their lives were going to change, and surely for the better. They didn't drink and spent about three weeks with his relatives before he landed a very good full-time position. This was the beginning of a bountiful life. Rose was focused on her husband and their new family, which soon included a second child. Rose wanted to be the perfect wife and mother and says she was "very conscientious about her children in their early years."

Rose also found alcohol to be the perfect ally when she was nervous about attending a social event. All the men drank, but the women didn't. Her drinking seemed to be tolerated, but it didn't really matter because she could stop anytime she chose. The first and only person who commented on her drinking at that time was her husband. This was certainly undue criticism as far as Rose was concerned. Wasn't *he* the person who drank so that he could slide past life's difficulties with ease? He was also the one who had taken a lover whose husband called Rose asking if she would join him in confronting the "couple" at a restaurant. This was the man who had the nerve to tell her *she* was drinking too much?

Although she hadn't been in contact with her family in a very long time, she decided to call her mom for advice. Her mom suggested that perhaps Rose should stop drinking and begin to take care of herself. Rose was not sure how she even knew. Soon after this conversation, Rose received news that her mother had had an aneurysm and passed away two days later. She returned to England for the funeral and managed to medicate considerably with alcohol and tranquilizers in order to fight through the devastation.

Back in Canada, the family moved again to a different province. As before, it was that geographic step that offered the false hope of a new beginning. Rose's husband always traveled but never forgot to bring back gifts. One gift Rose remembers was a huge bottle of Grand Marnier; this particular gift led to her first blackout. The police were called, and she was taken to the hospital, but she had hidden the bottle so well that no one ever found it. Even Rose was impressed with her ability to tuck away her liquor, and hiding it almost became an obsession. As her husband became more successful, their homes became a bigger and a pool was added, thus providing more places to secrete bottles.

Even Rose was impressed with her ability to tuck away her liquor, and hiding it almost became an obsession.

Rose's drinking was now totally out of control. She began making late-night long-distance calls to her brothers and father in the United Kingdom as well as to a young man she barely knew. She was feeling low so she went on antidepressants. A holiday in Mexico with the in-laws raised more than one comment. She was introduced to tequila, and the trip consisted of constant drinking and blackouts. Her children, who were with her in Mexico, were now at an age when they began to be disgusted by their mother's behavior. It would be years before her son told her how she had ruined that particular holiday for everyone. Like any alcoholic, Rose thought no one noticed her behavior or that they forgot it as quickly as she did.

The more Rose denied her disease, the more she drank. Yet she somehow found a way to earn a degree so that she could teach in Canada. Her intentions came to nothing, though, when her husband got extremely drunk and threw her belongings out after she would not comply with his sexual demands. Instead of fighting for herself and choosing to stop drinking and keep moving toward her career goal, she gave in to her addiction. Today she knows that she blamed him, but the reality was that as an alcoholic, Rose no longer had any choice. Drinking was the easier, softer way. Like any addict, Rose was not aware of the havoc alcohol had wreaked on both her body and soul.

Rose was also under the delusion that she was a marvelous mother and that her children should love and worship her. After all, she shuttled them and their friends to and from events—as if that was all it took to be a good mom. The truth was that after her children left for college and Rose was able to immerse herself fully in drinking, they would return home despising their mother for the "lowlife" she had become.

The truth was that after her children left for college and Rose was able to immerse herself fully in drinking, they would return home despising their mother for the "lowlife" she had become.

She couldn't stop drinking, so she told herself she didn't want to stop drinking. There is a certain amount of enjoyment in feeling numb. Surprisingly, Rose was able to hold down what she called "a simply heavenly job at a butterfly conservatory" and became a master of disguise. One day she was driving to work and had a seizure. She didn't have an accident but found she was almost disappointed she didn't die. From that point on, Rose cried quite a bit about how no one cared and began to have "accidents" at home like cutting her wrists, stomach, and breasts. Her self-loathing became a "now see what you make of this" attitude toward her family. Nothing happened. No one intervened, and so she became more and more the family joke. But Rose was not done yet. The swimming pool was a great prop! Her daughter fished her out more than once. Her husband and son enjoyed tormenting her by going on a "mommy's booze hunt" and would find the hidden bottles and pour the contents down the sink in front of her. Restraining her only seemed to add to their enjoyment. Oddly enough, from the outside, they continued on as though nothing was amiss. Weekend barbeques with family and friends were still on the calendar.

> *Rose's self-loathing became a "now see what you make of this" attitude toward her family.*

Rose says that she actually cannot recall one single "high point" during her drinking career. The lows were many. She tells me she lived her days for the love of alcohol, worshipping it as her god. She began drinking every day and used her best cut crystal. About the only thoughts that went through her head were about drinking: where to get it, when to get it, where to hide it, and calculating exactly how much she would need to tide her over on a weekend or holiday.

There were probably a number of bottoms during all these years of drinking, but Rose tells me that what she thought of as her bottom was when she fell down the concrete basement stairs for the last time (obviously, she had done it before). She broke two ribs, but nobody cared. Rose was in the hospital but, at that time, didn't feel worthy of care.

Her daughter had had enough. Unbeknownst to Rose, she approached a family-counseling center. Rose says that until recently, she had always felt that she was responsible for getting herself into recovery, but the truth is her recovery was due to her daughter's unflinching love for what remained of her mother.

Rose went to detox from the hospital, but there was a final suicide attempt. She took handfuls of the medication at the detox facility. She woke up after two days, alone and still alive but completely broken because she hadn't succeeded in ending it. She was taken to a rehab facility, and at that point, Rose had absolutely no fight left in her and no intention of picking up a drink ever again. She was prepared to do whatever it took to get sober and stay sober, and she began to see a glimmer of that light called hope.

Rose's recovery was due to her daughter's unflinching love for what remained of her mother.

The rehab was an all-women's facility, and she was there for almost four months. She left two days before Christmas with a diploma and a great deal of information and support. She would finally experience her first sober Christmas and the beginning of a new life.

Rose believes there have been quite a few miracles in her life since sobriety, and she has not relapsed since rehab. She would be the first to say that she has to remain vigilant because every now and then that feeling of melancholy creeps in. But she shares those feelings with her daughter, who has been with her every step of the way.

Recovery has meant working the 12 Steps in her life every single day. Although she has enjoyed sobriety for almost six years now, Rose feels that she is only beginning to truly touch recovery mentally, spiritually, and physically. Recovery has also meant changing other aspects of her life. Rose made the decision to separate from her husband and also to seek abuse counseling. There were lawyers, court hearings, moving into a small apartment, and having to deal with finances to get through. These are things she never had to do before, but she says she was "constantly guided to do the right things."

"I can step outside and hear the birds, smell the flowers, hear exquisite music, feel compassion— all so simple but indescribable. It takes my breath away and is the true glory of something far greater than ourselves."

The most beautiful gift in Rose's sobriety is her grandson. Today, Rose tells me, "I can step outside and hear the birds, smell the flowers, hear exquisite music, feel compassion—all so simple but indescribable. It takes my breath away and is the true glory of something far greater than ourselves.

"I now understand the true meaning of unconditional love and giving—I do the best I can. I know I am able to be of value to someone who shares my addiction and can share my own experience and guidance into 12-Step recovery. The decision has to be theirs."

Connie

Nothing is predestined. The obstacles of your past can
become the gateway to new beginnings.

—Ralph Blum

If you are in a 12-Step program of any type, you know that there are two distinct groups of people: newcomers and old-timers. The majority fall in the middle, and no one has ever stated exactly when you stop being labeled a "newcomer" and when you begin being labeled an "old-timer." I would say that at nineteen and a half years of sobriety, Connie might be classified as an "old-timer," although I'm not sure that this would be her first choice of words to describe herself. I hope that I will be able to give you a very clear picture of Connie not as an old-timer in recovery but as a woman who struggled with her addictions and found a solution sooner than many.

Connie is fifty-two and the divorced mom of two daughters. She is by far more fortunate than other family members because everyone in her family suffers from an addiction of one form or another. A few are in recovery, but up to this point, none have been able to stay sober for any length of time. Her oldest sister died of cirrhosis of the liver at the age of thirty-four. She knows her dad had a drinking problem, but today he is currently not drinking. He has not pursued any recovery groups to assist him in the process. Connie's ex-husband is also in recovery, and although he's not a blood relative, it is somewhat typical for addicts to be

It is somewhat typical for addicts to be attracted to other addicts. In some families it becomes a vicious cycle.

attracted to other addicts. In some families, it becomes a vicious cycle.

When you have an older brother and you want him to think you are very cool, you might want to do as he does. Connie was thought of as the "good girl," but by the time she was fourteen, she wasn't quite sure that appealed to her. She wanted to be bad and do something dangerous and so began smoking pot with her older brother so that he and his group of friends would accept her. She began drinking at this time also and immediately became not only a binger, but also a blackout drinker.

Connie was thought of as the "good girl," but by the time she was fourteen, she wasn't quite sure that appealed to her.

It didn't seem to be a problem. Connie could go without alcohol for long periods of time, but once she was introduced to marijuana, she found it difficult to go even one day without it.

Connie's time in high school was punctuated by smoking pot daily and drinking most weekends. It was all about drinking and blackouts on a regular basis. She was active in sports until her senior year, but that was interfering with her using. Fortunately, she was bright and her academics didn't suffer, but today Connie knows she could have accomplished so much more if she had not wasted so much of her time on pot and booze.

College came, and Connie continued her drinking and pot smoking. It was the '70s for heaven's sake, and didn't everyone do this? In retrospect, Connie knows that it was the grace of God that kept her safe and helped her graduate. After all these years of drinking and smoking, Connie was quite pleased that she hadn't graduated into any other drugs, because they certainly were all harder than pot.

She met her husband while she was in college. She had been friends with his sister in high school, and they had remained friends because they both had similar tastes in activities (partying). Connie also did a typical geographic shift from the East Coast to the Southwest. When she met her future husband, Mark, they were both engaged to different people. They were both in their early twenties and ended up not marrying those people. Connie said that their first date should have been a clue. They started drinking early in the day and then proceeded to take white crosses (speed) and ended up in a bar listening to a friend's band. Connie honestly doesn't remember most of the evening and got violently ill when she returned home. Today, she quietly laughs when she says "I think that's when Mark realized I was the one!"

Connie and Mark married, and their lives centered on drinking and drugging. Their friends were people who did the same thing. It was no longer about pot but rather cocaine and then crystal meth.

Connie had her first child when she was thirty and thought for sure that would straighten her out.

Connie had her first child when she was thirty and thought for sure that would straighten her out. She had to see a fertility specialist to even get pregnant and was very excited when she conceived. She only drank a little and did not use drugs during that period. When her child was about nine months old, Connie decided to "reward" herself for being so good. It was her birthday, and so she bought some crystal meth. She returned to full-time using. After that, everything went downhill, including her marriage.

It was easy to be in denial because although she was unhappy, depressed, and miserable, she didn't believe it was from her drinking or drug use. Like many alcoholics/addicts, she got into the blame game. It was her husband and the bad marriage or it was life's circumstances, and there was nothing she could do.

Connie was still functioning, so denial was easy. She had her daughter, a husband, a home, friends, and a job. It looked pretty good from the outside. But everything in her life revolved around whether or not she had enough drugs, how much she would be using that day, and what she was doing at the time. If she was high and had to go to work, she would try and appear normal and sober. A lot of energy went into the day-to-day acquiring, using, or not using, depending on the day and situation.

The average day involved getting up and working out, since exercise always made what you were doing not seem so bad. If Connie wasn't using street drugs, then she would take a combination of herbal uppers to get high and begin drinking as soon as she got home from work. If coke or meth was available, that would be great, but it depended on how much money she had at the time. She tells me that meth was much cheaper than coke and lasted longer, so that was definitely a front-runner. The drugs would hype her up, and she could stay up for days. She would drink whiskey to keep her hands from shaking so that she could do her job, which required manual dexterity and interacting with people. She had to keep up appearances.

All in all, Connie was having a difficult time being a mother and a drug addict. She spiraled down quickly after the birth of her daughter, but her bottom(s) were close at hand.

Connie tells me her bottom was a combination of things. The first was that moment of clarity that hits addicts and hopefully shines enough light on their issues for them to begin to question their behaviors. Connie's daughter was about two years old. Connie had been up for a couple of days. When her daughter woke up, all Connie could think was how "this poor girl had been born to a drug-addicted, alcoholic mother and that this beautiful little thing was headed for a horrible life." She didn't want to be that kind of parent.

The second moment involved her daughter around the same time. Connie had taken a week off to spend time with her but got so loaded the first night that she was sick the entire time. They did absolutely nothing. Connie hated herself the whole week and realized what she had become.

Connie wanted to get sober but was still not totally convinced it was all her. She had been in therapy before, but this time, because she worked for a company that had an employee-assistance program, she made an appointment to talk to a counselor about her home situation and her husband's alcohol and pot problem. The man she saw would not permit her to discuss her husband but asked about her own alcohol and drug use. He quickly convinced her she had a problem and that there was no such thing as a "social meth or cocaine user."

Connie's daughter was two when she began recovery. Mark followed, but the marriage was on again, off again. He was seeing other women, and Connie was just trying to stay sober. At one point they decided to give it another try. Connie honestly never thought she would get pregnant again. She had needed to go to a specialist for the first child. Today, she realizes part of her ease in getting pregnant the second time was because she had cleaned up her body. And so Connie gave birth to another daughter.

Her difficulties, however, were still coming, but not because of alcohol or drugs. Connie was severely depressed and ended up having something of a nervous breakdown.

She ended up going into a treatment program not only to handle her addictions but also to deal with some childhood issues. Having this second daughter seemed to bring everything to a head.

Connie's husband was very supportive, and with the help of both their sponsors, she entered thirty-day rehab. She was mortified at first that it would be so long, but looking back, she knows it was the best thing she could have done. She continued in some intense therapy but today can walk through the pain and move on.

Mark and Connie were married for fifteen years. They used together but also worked a recovery program together. They remained together about five years after they both got sober, but the marriage had gone through too much to survive. The good news is that Connie says that even though they ended up divorced, they stayed civil with each other and have a great relationship with each other and the girls.

Today, Connie remains very involved in a 12-Step program. She attends lots of meetings, sponsors other women, does service work, and has volunteered on various committees and events. This is how she protects herself against a relapse. "It's too easy to forget how bad it really was," Connie says.

"Everything I have learned about motherhood, friendship, work, and life I have learned in the rooms of my 12-Step recovery program."

She just took her "sober baby" (second daughter) to college this past week. "It has been a bittersweet journey growing up together. At least that is what it has felt like for most of our lives. I can say today that I believe sobriety made me a wonderful mother and peer to my girls. I didn't think that in the beginning, but through it all, I knew when to ask for help, which battles were worth fighting, and when they needed to be loved. Everything I have learned about motherhood, friendship, work, and life I have learned in the rooms of my 12-Step recovery program."

Connie believes that anyone in an addiction who wants to get sober and remain so has to find that power greater than oneself. It is not about religion. It's about going to meetings, getting a sponsor, and working the steps. If she could do it as a single mom with two kids and a job, you can't say you don't have time. If sobriety is a priority, you have to find the time.

To families or friends of someone addicted, Connie says that unless an alcoholic or addict wants help, there isn't much you can do other than protect yourself through a 12-Step program. Learn about boundaries and enabling.

Connie's mantra? One day at a time!

Mr. R

The safest way to double your money is to fold it over once and put it in your pocket.

—Kin Hubbard

Alcoholics and drug addicts are easy to come by. What I wanted and needed was someone addicted to gambling because I feel that the average person (including myself) doesn't really know much about compulsive gambling. I had the opportunity to interview someone who is not only a recovering gambler but is also in the business of helping others to recovery.

When I first met Mr. R, he said, "I can tell you a 30-, 60-, 90-, 120-, or 180-minute story." I told him to give me a short version but not to leave out anything. He had told his story so often he was able to do what I asked.

Mr. R describes himself as a "genetically predisposed addict." Both his paternal grandfather and his father were alcoholics. They were of the functional variety but alcoholics nonetheless. Given the choice as an adolescent between smoking a joint and taking a drink, he always chose the former. He was prone to hangovers and had seen the devastating effects of alcohol in this family. Gambling had not yet come into the picture.

Both of his parents were bridge players, his father accumulating "master points," and they spent a couple of nights every week playing with friends. There were also games on Saturday nights that would rotate from home to home. By the time Mr. R was twelve or thirteen years old, he could play bridge better than most kids his age. Little did he know that this would be the beginning of his career as a gambler.

High school was an all-male prep school that Mr. R thought of at the time as a reformatory where he had been sent due to a conspiracy between his parents and their minister. In retrospect, he realizes he got an academically superior high school education. He also determined that he was the second-best bridge player on that campus and so, teamed with the best bridge player on campus, wound up taking as much money from the rich kids at school as he could. Mr. R was not one of those rich kids. His mother had even gone back to work to be able to afford his education. Mr. R calls this his "first gambling of significance" and the start of the first of the three phases of this addiction, called the winning phase. Mr. R was sixteen.

After graduating from the prep school, he went off to a big-city university and says he "majored in drug addiction." This meant any drug anybody put in front of him that he could smoke, eat, or snort. Unlike many of his friends, he did have an aversion to putting a needle in his arm. He experimented with acid twice, but after one of his suite mates jumped off a fifteen-story building while on acid, he decided that acid was not the drug for him. He smoked marijuana, however, the way other people smoked cigarettes.

He transferred to another school and began using amphetamines. He thought it was helping him study, but he ended up going to a hospital to detox. It was there that he met the woman who later would become his wife (now ex-wife).

It was summertime, and Mr. R was working at a rock-and-roll nightclub when a buddy asked him if he wanted to go to the horse races. Now, he knew enough to wager a win, place, or show but didn't know how to "exotically wager," as he puts it. They won. He still remembers the exact amount: $376.40 apiece. He says he remembers it as if it was five minutes ago because that is what he still refers to from a clinical perspective as the "hook." This experience crystallized the gambling addiction, because he was not chasing the money. He was chasing the feeling. He realized he did not have to work for a living. Oh, and another somewhat important event: He got married.

Within three months, he resigned his job, read three books on Thoroughbred handicapping, and was at the racetrack every day. He was betting $500 a week, which he felt was still somewhat under control. But his marriage was suffering because he spent each and every night looking at the racing forms to prepare for the following day. This was his job!

His wife went to visit her family for Christmas, and she didn't come back. They separated, but Mr. R still played the horses. Finally, she said she would return to the marriage if he would get a real job. "I'm done with all this crazy gambling stuff," she told him.

So he did find a job in a corporation that just happened to be about three miles from the track. This was rather convenient because he could sneak over at least three to four times a week. She thought he was going once a week by the time he had started going five.

Discovery! Bookmakers! Betting sports! Because Mr. R went to a school known for ice hockey, he thought he was an expert in that sport, but he also bet on baseball, football, and basketball.

The problem was that Mr. R was moving from the winning phase of his addiction to the losing phase. The bank account was getting lower and lower, the credit card debt was just beginning to show, and the cash flow was now negative on a weekly basis. His winning phase had lasted only about one year.

But the corporate job was working out well, and he was offered a promotion in another city. He took the promotion and the transfer. What Mr. R remembers most about this is that on the very first day he and his wife arrived in their new home, they stayed in a hotel. She was going to go back and pack and make the move while he worked. Neither of them knew a single soul in this city, but he told her he had a meeting with his boss. He didn't. He was going to the racetrack and left her sitting alone in a hotel room.

The bookmakers continued, and the horse racing continued. The promotions did, also. The couple transferred to the West Coast, and they were now very close to Las Vegas. Now, in all this time, Mr. R had never been to Vegas, and one his work friends suggested a weekend trip. When he arrived in Vegas, he described it as "Valhalla," and so subconsciously, yet consciously, he set his sights on being a professional gambler.

He eventually moved even closer to Vegas so that he could go as much as possible, and because of that, the quality of his work suffered. He quit right before he was fired. There wasn't anything to worry about though, because by this time his marriage had ended in divorce and he had discovered cocaine. The combination of gambling and cocaine was just about perfect.

The combination of gambling and cocaine was just about perfect.

Mr. R now had a live-in girlfriend who worked every day while he continued to go to the racetrack or back and forth to Vegas. This went on for about four and a half years. He next describes moving into the chase and desperation phase of his addiction. The credit cards were now being maxed out, so he got more credit cards and maxed them out, and so on. He had found a partner to help shop sports lines and get the best prices for sporting events. He was also convinced he could become a professional card counter at blackjack. He was good enough at this to be asked to leave several casinos. The truth is, as Mr. R tells me, his mathematical ability had actually started out quite good but was compromised by the addiction. Horse racing, by the way, had lost its appeal.

The live-in girlfriend was accepted into a doctoral program in the Midwest, and this created a good excuse to leave Vegas and get away from certain people now looking for him. So they moved, but it would be two more years of gambling before Mr. R went to a 12-Step recovery meeting for gamblers. Why? The relationship ended. She had left him for the fifth time and this time had changed the locks. He couldn't get a set of keys. He hated her therapist because she wouldn't let her talk to him. He had been fired now from two jobs for stealing, had a car that had no heater and was worth about $600, and felt he was at an emotional, spiritual, and financial bottom.

Mr. R had been fired now from two jobs for stealing, had a car that had no heater and was worth about $600, and felt he was at an emotional, spiritual, and financial bottom.

Mr. R went to ninety meetings in ninety days, wasn't using cocaine, and wasn't gambling in that period. But he admits he wasn't even close to really pursuing recovery. A very bad thing happened: He got the highest-paying job he would ever have!

The money threw him into the delusion that his problems had been financial all along and that he was just fine emotionally and spiritually. Mr. R grew financially healthy quickly, but he still owed money to certain people. One important step that came out of the recovery meetings he attended was that a meeting was set up between him and the men he owed. A deal, so to speak, was made. The real significance of this meeting, however, was to encourage abstinence from gambling. Mr. R took this seriously and followed up at least with gambling.

The cocaine was gone, gambling was history, so how did he feel? Mr. R had an aversion to alcohol early on, but that's what was left. He drank at an alcoholic level for at least a year and a half. The corporation with that great job was sold. He moved to the South. His father had recently had a stroke, and so he thought that might be a good place to land.

Within two months of moving near his father, Mr. R got a DUI. This was one of those blessings in disguise. "Finally some consequences," he told me. What Mr. R had forgotten to mention to me earlier in his story was that he had a felony charge on the books for running an illegal gambling casino years earlier. There were some political strings pulled at that time, and so although the felony stuck, there were no other consequences. Until now.

He was forced to attend 12-Step meetings for recovering alcoholics and forced into private therapy as an alternative to DUI-ordered therapy. The combination of meetings every night and therapy seemed to be working. The only thing that didn't work was Mr. R finding his new girlfriend in the meeting room very early on, although he was advised by his sponsor that "this is a fellowship of people trying to stop drinking. This is not a dating club." Mr. R didn't pay much attention to his sponsor but

He rode up and down on the elevator trying to decide whether he should stay with his dying mom on the third floor or with his girlfriend in emergency.

learned later the hard truth about dating someone early in sobriety.

Then came what Mr. R calls the "toughest day of my life." His mom was dying of lung cancer, and his dad was coping by getting drunk. Mr. R was spending about eighteen hours a day at the hospital sitting with his mom. When he came home one evening, he found that his girlfriend had OD'd. He called an ambulance, and they took her to the same hospital as his mom. For the next three hours, he said he rode up and down on the elevator trying to decide whether he should stay with his dying mom on the third floor or with his girlfriend in emergency. He prayed, "God, you told me that you would never give me more than I could handle, but tonight you are really pushing the envelope."

The girlfriend had a blood-alcohol content of .0455. She lived. His mom died that night. He got his dad into detox, and his girlfriend went into recovery. Mr. R said, "I finally started to get real serious about my recovery."

Serious he was: He ended up buying a duplex for himself and his dad and gave up half of the space to guys new to sobriety from alcohol and gambling. Throughout the years, Mr. R had taken money from his parents and was now resolved to paying back every single penny. Although his father thought it foolish since Mr. R was an only child and would end up with whatever money there was anyway, he explained that paying back the money was important to his recovery. His father accepted that, and that's the way it was for at least three and a half years until Mr. R says that the day came when their roles were flipped. He had now become the parent and by the grace of God could manage the money responsibly. Mr. R's dad, who had been drinking all his life, detoxed after his wife's death when he was seventy-nine years old. He was sober when he died at ninety-two. I ask Mr. R how his dad stayed sober. He laughs. "Not because he wanted to but because he stopped driving. I wouldn't buy him liquor. He wasn't within walking distance of the liquor store, and I did all his grocery shopping. He got dry at least."

Today, Mr. R not only works a personal 12-Step program but is also instrumental in working with other gamblers and their families. He is also very happily married. Oh, and before I forget, he gave up cigarettes about six years ago, but that's another story for another day!

Beverly

We love our habits more than our income, often more than our life.

—Bertrand Russell

There are two reasons why Beverly intrigued me. First of all, she is seventy-five and the oldest of all the people I talked to and interviewed for this book and has been sober only five years. If there is any lesson to be found in "better late than never," Beverly has learned it and learned it well. The second thing that is interesting is that Beverly was a softball player. So in my mind, I see Beverly out there in *A League of Their Own*, and I just have to smile.

I believe that when you read Bev's story you have to put yourself into a time that was a bit tough on women and certainly less accepting of an alcoholic woman. She had a hard life but hard in a different way than what we would have today. I don't think that drinking was any different then than it is now, but the support in recovery is significantly better today. It took Bev a very long time, but as she told me, "My name is Beverly. I am an alcoholic who tried to quit drinking and finally did."

If there is any lesson to be found in "better late than never," Beverly has learned it and learned it well.

Beverly chose to tell her story as we sometimes do in recovery. We divide our lives into "what it was like," "what happened," and "what it is like now." I have chosen to keep that format here.

What it was like: Bev says, "It was hell!" She was raised by a single mom because her dad took off when she was about three weeks old. She never saw him and had no desire to.

Her mom remarried and had two boys. Life was actually good, and they did so many things as a family. Bev started school, and all was well until ... one of her brothers became very sick with meningitis. In those days, there wasn't anything to be done medically. He got worse and died at the age of four.

Bev's mom took it very hard, but life went on. Her stepdad went to work each day, and her mom stayed home. There wasn't a lot of money in the household, and so as she was growing up, Beverly did jobs for neighbors like cleaning snow off of the sidewalk. It was the only way she could get a little spending money and also lunch money. The year was 1946, and times were hard. She remembers being at her grandparents' and buying sugar with stamps and having a sticker on the windshield of the car in order to buy gas.

Every summer Beverly would go to her grandparents' house. Then one summer the unthinkable happened. Beverly was sexually abused by an uncle. She never mentioned it to anyone, not even her mother. She questioned whether it was her fault or not.

Her mother and stepfather were divorced when she was twelve, and by that time she was old enough to babysit her brother when her mom had to return to work. Her mom got married again to a man whom Beverly absolutely hated. At fourteen, Beverly was sexually abused for the second time. Once again she didn't tell anyone because she didn't want anyone, especially her mom, to think badly of her, and once again, she asked herself, "What the hell is wrong with me?" She would not realize until recovery that stifling her emotions about this abuse and the earlier episode of abuse in her life would have cast a pall over her entire life.

The second marriage produced a lot of domestic violence, so after the divorce, Beverly had kind of had it and moved away from home at eighteen. She joined a softball team, and that brought her first taste of alcohol.

What happened: "This is where it all started," says Beverly. "What better way to enjoy a beer than after a ballgame." The more games she played, the more alcohol she drank. The drinking kept getting worse and worse until she made the typical geographic ploy tried by most addicts of going to another city, thinking things would get better. They never do. As Beverly puts it, "Where I go, there I am." She began working in this new city and within no time at all had totaled a car, run over a motorcycle, and driven into a building.

Within no time at all, she had totaled a car, run over a motorcycle, and driven into a building.

She decided to go back home to visit her mom and on the way got a DUI. She was too drunk to know what city she was in. She spent twenty-four hours in jail and paid some fairly big fines. She topped that off by "relaxing" by a pool (actually, she passed out) in the hot sun and burned herself to a crisp. Beverly's own words are "Anyone in their right mind would have quit after that." But she didn't.

Her mother died, and her brother also passed away. She made all kinds of promises to people that she would quit drinking and had what she called the "emergency God"—the one you ask to get you out of a situation and, if so, promise you will never do it again.

But drinking continued twenty-four hours a day, 7 days a week, 365 days a year, and to the point where she was not afraid of dying. "I was afraid of living," she tells me. After all this, she still thought she could stop if she wanted to. Through the years, others certainly saw the drinking and its devastating effects, and they did mention it to her. Beverly tells me that when someone would comment on her drinking, it really "pissed me off," and the more they mentioned it, the more she drank. One of the biggest reasons she did not want to stop was this: "I could be someone important (when I drank). I was noticed."

"I was afraid of living."

Somewhere along the line (Beverly really doesn't go into detail), she did get sober and stayed sober for a number of years. She was part of a 12-Step program, went to meetings, did service work, volunteered, worked the steps, shared at meetings, and, in her words, "had it all going on." During this period of time, she met a woman who was quite lonely. Beverly was also lonely, and they became friends. Beverly says that "things progressed from there," and she is now Beverly's partner.

One day, for no real reason, Beverly took a drink. She continued going to meetings and would stop at the local Walgreens, get a sixteen-ounce soda, and mix it with vodka. She thought no one could smell it. It is almost impossible to go to a meeting with a group of alcoholics and think you could hide a drink. Contrary to popular belief, vodka does have a smell!

This went on for a while until one day someone decided to take a stand on the situation. Her partner told her to "either clean up your act or hit the highway." Beverly finally made the decision to get clean and stay clean. She went into a detox facility for three days and then went to a ninety-day women's residential inpatient facility. She did everything she was told to do, but a week after she left the facility, she drank again and got another DUI. That was her last taste of alcohol. She went back to rehab a second time, where she was able to work through her past, specifically her sexual molestations. She realizes that she could not deal with the reality of those experiences, and drinking had allowed her to forget. All the emotions surfaced during treatment so she could face them, and she is now five years sober.

How it is now: "God gave me a second chance. The little things that used to piss me off are of no significance to me today." Beverly goes to a 12-Step meeting every single day. If she doesn't, she says her "whole day is shot." She is very active in fellowship history and archive research and has put together all her findings to display for a Founders' Day. She is quite proud of that. "So you see, my life has come full circle. My sponsor told me my sobriety depends on how high you bounce once you hit bottom." Beverly has, today, hit the heights!

> *"God gave me a second chance. The little things that used to piss me off are of no significance to me today."*

Lori

> *The truth is we are not yet free; we have merely achieved the freedom to be free.*
>
> —Nelson Mandela

The timing couldn't have been more perfect for me. An article appeared in the local newspaper about a young woman who was preparing to graduate from college. The "big story," so to speak, was that Dana was a high school dropout and a drug addict. At the age of twenty-three, she had already been in recovery for five years. A very good "lost and found" story, as I have come to call these.

I wanted to hear her mom's story, though. Addicts are often more agreeable about telling their stories than the parent or spouse of the addicted person is. There are a number of reasons for such reluctance. Family members can feel responsible for and somewhat embarrassed about the path the addict has taken. In many cases, they were enablers and feel uncomfortable with their part in the addiction. So when I was able to get in touch with this mother, Lori, and she was willing to give me her version, I was delighted.

This may be less of a chronology of events because it was more of a conversation with Lori. There are a few questions, and then Lori takes off from there.

So let's begin with the family unit as Dana was growing up. Lori and her husband were married for twenty-six years before they divorced. They had four children, with three in three years. Dana was the second. Lori describes her marriage as "very difficult" from Day One. The last child, who is ten years younger than the third, was "kind of a Band-Aid that didn't work." So from the beginning, the home may not have been dysfunctional but was certainly uncomfortable.

Lori says that of all her children, Dana was the perfect pregnancy and the easiest baby. She amused herself and read books when she was older. Absolutely perfect. She was everything a parent could ask for, but she was also the kind that did her own thing; after she and her siblings were dressed and ready to go out, for example, she would suddenly say "I don't want to wear this!" and would be adamant about changing clothes. Lori says then that everyone said, "Oh, she's going to be trouble!"

When she went to middle school, she was on the student council and the honor roll and played sports. In high school, she was still enrolled in honors classes, was in jazz band and captain of the softball team, and seemed happy.

Then somewhere in her sophomore year, it began. She started changing. She went from this cute little blond girl to dark makeup and dyeing her hair black—the goth thing—and she dropped out of softball and band. Dana went out all the time, and no one could seem to control her.

I ask Lori what was going through her mind when these changes began, and like most parents of teenagers, she simply thought it was a stage. Lori honestly believed that Dana's change in appearance was teenage rebellion but also that Dana was going to get high at some point in her teenage years. Lori thought that she should just do all that stuff now: Like most kids she would maybe get high (probably marijuana), drink a little, and then grow up and be done with it.

Lori thought that she should just do all that stuff now: Like most kids she would maybe get high (probably marijuana), drink a little, and then grow up and be done with it.

Lori had no reason to believe that there were any drugs or alcohol involved at that point, but Dana's appearance and behavior was a source of embarrassment leading to denial. The family lived in a very affluent area, and Lori was worried about people talking. Actually, they were buzzing. All Lori could think was "I can't control my child. It's not my fault." After all, Lori and her husband were going through an extremely bad time, and he was never around, so Lori had to face the lion's share of Dana's problems.

By the time Dana was a junior, Lori still wasn't sure about the drugs (denial, she said) but decided that Dana was giving her too many reasons not to trust her. She was staying out late, Lori didn't know any of her friends, and when Dana was home, she isolated herself. She went into Dana's room and found marijuana and glue in her dresser drawer. She confronted Dana, who fully admitted that they were hers.

For whatever reason, Lori went to Dana's high school and told her counselor she was using. Lori wanted to pull her out of this school and send her to a different one in the same district with a somewhat reciprocal understanding if a student chose one over the other. Lori phoned the second high school and told the principal why she wanted a transfer for Dana. He okayed it. When she approached the first school, the principal said he would permit the transfer if Dana would give him the names of all the drug dealers at the school. Lori was incensed and said, "For God's sake! She is sixteen years old. She's not going to tell me or anyone." The principal looked at her and said, "Well, I guess I'm not going to sign a transfer." Lori could not believe what she was hearing. It was blackmail. That's when Lori said she would just pull Dana out of high school, and she did. By the way, the principal is no longer at that school.

Lori knows that she does not know everything about Dana's life as an addict. She is not sure she wants to.

Lori didn't care how high Dana was: She was going to study and take the GED. About halfway through the exam, Dana came out and said, "I'm done with this, and I'm leaving. I'll come back." Lori dug her heels in and told her daughter, "If you leave, don't come back." Dana went back in and took the rest of the GED and passed it. The reason Lori tells this story is that she felt there were times she *did* put her foot down. She admits she is not an assertive person, "but there have been a few instances that I have put my foot down and I think, gosh, that works!"

Lori knows that she does not know everything about Dana's life as an addict. She is not sure she wants to. There are incidents that Dana brings up today that Lori has no memory of. There are things Lori recalls but admits she isn't sure what order they happened in exactly. All she can tell me is that they did happen.

Dana wasn't really into alcohol so much as drugs. Early on in this nightmare, she had come home drunk enough that Lori had taken her to the ER for alcohol poisoning. She had had an entire bottle of vodka on the bus ride home from a band concert, but Lori doesn't think alcohol was the issue. It was the drugs. This is the scary part: Heroin is sometimes easier for a kid under eighteen to get than beer.

Heroin is sometimes easier for a kid under eighteen to get than beer.

Dana went into rehab a couple of times. Lori says that one in particular was like camp. They did IOP (intensive outpatient) on Tuesdays, and the families would join them on Thursdays. Dana told her mom that sitting right across the circle from her was her drug dealer, and after the meetings, they would go into the parking lot and get high.

On Dana's eighteenth birthday, after she had stayed out all night, Lori told her daughter that she could no longer live at home. Lori said she just couldn't deal with it anymore. She couldn't deal with the hurt. So Dana left but called Lori one day at work and asked for help. Lori told her to call her sponsor and get whatever she needed. (Dana had been to enough recovery meetings to have gotten a sponsor.) For Lori, this was a turning point. She says that she has heard her share of parents saying "I could never turn my back on my child" or "I could never let my child be on the streets. Never." Lori says she looks at them and wants to say "You know what? There was a period of time when if someone would have taken her from me, I would have been happy. I couldn't get rid of her. I called the police. I would call help lines. I would say that I didn't want her in my house anymore. I've got a six-year-old and I've got syringes filled with heroin. Take her." When Lori would say this out loud to anyone in authority or anyone who would listen and maybe help, they would respond with something like "We're really sorry, but you can put her on your back patio and give her food, but you are stuck with her." It all sounds so terrible today, and Lori says it was such a weird feeling, but she just wanted her to go away. It was too much, and Lori was on overload.

It all sounds so terrible today, but Lori just wanted Dana to go away.

Someone Lori knew also had a daughter who was using. The mom found syringes, and the daughter admitted everything. She told Lori she didn't know what to do, and when Lori told the mom to make her leave the house, the mom said, "Well, she has court and this, and that, and if I do, she will be in trouble." "You know what?" Lori says, "At what point do you just not say a word?"

When Dana was about fifteen, she took the car and was arrested for drunk driving. She called Lori in the middle of the night from the police station. Lori knew Dana would have to go to court and prepared her for a hefty fine as well as jail. Then the judge gave her fifteen hours of community service, and Lori said, "Are you kidding me?"

When they released Dana that same night, she went out and used again because she didn't even remember that she had died and been brought back.

One of the worst memories Lori has as a parent, and something that only an addict would understand, was Dana's experience with speedballs (injections of cocaine and heroin). She was with two guys, and when Dana passed out, they couldn't wake her. They put her in the car and dropped her off at an ER. She flatlined and was not breathing. The ER called Lori, of course. When they released Dana that same night, she went out and used again because she didn't even remember that she had died and been brought back.

Then Dana was arrested for heroin possession and had to spend the night in jail. The following morning Lori picked her up, although she says she really didn't want to. She knew if she didn't, Dana would be turned over to Child Protective Services. Dana's court date was in May, the same time Lori's son was graduating. Dana went before the judge, and he looked at Lori and her husband (yes, he was there) and said, "I don't think you parents can control your daughter." Dana went to jail. They were able to get her a twenty-four-hour pass to attend her brother's graduation, but then Dana spent three weeks in jail. That judge knew what he was doing, Lori felt. Lori says that Dana will tell her that one of the things that keeps her clean today is that she doesn't want to go back to jail ... ever. It left a lasting impression on her.

When she was ready, Dana went to detox and rehab. Today Dana works a 12-Step recovery program and goes to meetings. She tells Lori that sometimes it seems "unfair" that at her age she can't have a drink with her friends. Lori tells her that life is all about choices, and today she is much better prepared to make the right ones. Dana is hoping to enter law school. She has such a full life right in front of her!

What about Lori? Lori is now a proud mom and wouldn't change anything she did for a second. She empathizes with parents who have young addicted kids. She tells me that no one realizes that if your child is under eighteen it is one of the most difficult things you can ever imagine. Lori tells me she thinks it is extremely important for the parents to work together and not put the blame on themselves or each other. Lori did the tough love thing because she had no choice. It worked for her. Lori does not attend any type of 12-Step meetings for herself, but she has not ruled them out either.

"With everything that happened, with all we have gone through, I look around and know that I am one of the lucky ones!"

Lori's future, like Dana's, is all about choices. Lori has been through a lot but says "With everything that happened, with all we have gone through, I look around and know that I am one of the lucky ones!"

Sandy

You can search the whole universe and not find a single being more worthy of love than yourself. Since each and every person is so precious to themselves, let the self-respecting harm no other being.

—Buddha

Sandy was four when she was introduced to the person and the thing that would springboard her into addiction.

They called him "Happy Earl," and he drove a big semi. He was the person who quietly fondled Sandy at least once and then had the nerve to ask if she liked it. She was four years old, for heaven's sake, and she said no. She is not clear if this happened more than once, but regardless, she told no one. Later on she found out that Happy Earl had had a twenty-five-year affair with her grandma, and everyone knew about it, including grandpa. Happy Earl was no gentleman!

The "thing" was Nyquil. Sandy was spending the night with her grandparents and was not feeling well. They gave her Nyquil—not Children's Nyquil, but adult Nyquil. She says she was instantly addicted, and each and every time she spent a night at her grandparents' house, she would invariably have a cough, cold, or sore throat. She knew then that she could manipulate the situation to get Nyquil, and she did. Grandpa also imbibed spirits and sipped on rum and Coke every night of the week. For years he shared his drink with her.

It really doesn't seem like Sandy had a fighting chance to live a sober life. Her father was a heroin addict. As Sandy tells it, "My mom was in her teens when they got married. She did not marry a heroin addict; he at least waited until I was conceived. Then he became a real junkie." Sandy tells me that her dad would shoot up in front of her and take her to trailer parks and gross places. Sandy's childhood photos include one picture of her sitting on top of a twenty-pound brick of marijuana and another of her surrounded by beer bottles.

Sandy's childhood photos include one picture of her sitting on top of a twenty-pound brick of marijuana.

While her young mom worked at a bank and brought home little money, her dad worked at various jobs to support his addiction. But, as Sandy puts it, "When heroin was in town (and that was most of the time), my dad was a junkie, a robber, and a dealer. He wasn't a really nice guy." Her mom was in denial. He told her that if she ever left him, he would die. She didn't, but "God took care of that," says Sandy.

It was not unusual for the police to come knocking at the door of their very small cottage to arrest her dad. Sandy could not help but hear and see it all because she slept in the kitchen. Her dad was definitely not a stranger to the local jail, and Sandy remembers visiting him there often. She doesn't recall it as a jail cell but as an office. She isn't sure if that was because he was a "regular" and they knew him or if it was for her benefit because she was so young.

The last time the police came to the door, something was different. This time when Sandy's mom said, "He is not home," the police responded, "Yes. We know. That's why we are here." Sandy peeked around the corner and heard the officer explaining that her dad would not be coming home. He was dead. It was ruled a homicide.

Sandy's mom never told her the truth. They never talked about it. Sandy says she did not bring it up because she was afraid that it would hurt her mom's feelings. At the funeral, the first for the six-year-old, her mom cried, and Sandy says it was one of the first times she had ever seen her mom do that. Sandy felt sad and didn't know how to talk about it and anyway had no one to talk to.

A big part of Sandy's story is her mother's denial about anything and everything. Even at this young age, Sandy realized her mom was just acting as if nothing was happening. Later on Sandy found out that when her mom was eight months pregnant with her, she insisted she didn't know she was pregnant. Sandy believes this accounts for the lack of nurturing from her mom and their very disconnected relationship. There was never bonding of any type. She felt a lot closer to her grandma. The saddest part of Sandy's childhood was that she says she didn't know how to be a child. She had so many questions as well as shame. "I was just a lost child," she tells me.

She had this longing, a burning desperation for someone to wrap their arms around her and tell her everything was going to be okay. Nobody did.

At the age of seven, her mom remarried, and the family moved to a different state. Life was better.

Her stepdad was a good man, and today she loves him and thinks he is a hero. But at that time, Sandy says she was just pissed. Her mom never hugged her, kissed her, or showed love to her because she didn't know how, yet Sandy could see how much her mom loved her stepdad. Sandy believes this is the beginning of her love addiction. She had this longing, a burning desperation for someone to wrap their arms around her and tell her everything was going to be okay. Nobody did. Her stepdad did the best he could, but as Sandy recalls, "He was the stepdad, and you don't wrap your arms around a little girl when you are some dude. It's creepy!"

The next few years were good for the entire family. Sandy became interested in gymnastics and was good enough to be ranked in the state. At thirteen she injured her knee badly enough that her gymnastic future hung in the balance. Sandy says that her parents, coach, and surgeon all sat down with her and gave her a choice. She could continue gymnastics after surgery, rehab, and a lot of time, or she could decide the gymnastics was over. Sandy chose the latter. She didn't want to do it any longer. She was thirteen, going into junior high, and she saw a different life ahead of her.

Oh, it was different all right! Within a very short period of time, Sandy started smoking marijuana, did mushrooms, dropped acid, experimented with angel dust, and began staying out all night and having sex. All her seventh-grade friends did the same.

I ask Sandy about her friends, and she tells me that if they did all the drugs she did, they were her friends. Many of her friends were older, particularly her boyfriends. When she was seventeen, her boyfriend was twenty-seven!

When she was twenty, her boyfriend was forty-five. She believes that this is the "older man" syndrome: the father who can take care of you because you don't think you can do it on your own. Sandy tells me that she didn't know what age she was when she decided that if she had an older man, he would never leave. She would always be younger and prettier.

Sandy only chose boyfriends who drank and did drugs. They always had money for drugs, specifically cocaine, which had become Sandy's drug of choice. She liked to be "kept." The boyfriends took her on trips and bought her jewelry. Her drinking and drugging progressed rapidly. Sandy was still in high school.

After graduation Sandy went to beauty school. It was what she had dreamed of since she had been a little girl. She also started to hang out with a girl who had come from a different high school and became a best friend. Sandy had a whole new group of friends as she partied and did cocaine all through beauty school. Still, she graduated and was good at what she did.

The best friend ended up dying of a brain aneurysm later on. Sandy says it was probably drug related. The hard part, though, was that the girl's mom would not let Sandy visit her, so when she died, there was no closure. The same thing happened to another friend whom she had known since her teen years. His parents would not let Sandy see him in the hospital.

Just like when her dad was murdered, no one would talk about it. Secrets. Always secrets. It was almost as if they thought Sandy was too fragile to handle the truth, and because she felt these secrets hanging over her, she thought she would just do more drugs.

I ask Sandy if her parents knew of her alcohol and drug abuse, and she believes they did but thought that she would grow out of it. If they had tried to do anything at all or confronted her with it, Sandy is pretty sure she would only have been angry.

Sandy was (and still is) a creative, talented stylist and at the age of twenty was hired at a high-end salon. The owner became her boyfriend, and because of this affair, he sold the salon. Sandy had no choice but to get another position. It was easy. She worked in a salon that did massive hair shows and fashion shows for upscale department stores. The real perk for Sandy was that the booze and coke kept flying at these shows. It was accepted in the industry, so why not? And that is what Sandy did for the next twenty-three years. She drank, used cocaine, and styled hair!

There were times Sandy had to take a backseat to a drug deal, but as long as this guy continued to buy her clothes and jewelry and put her up in high-class resorts with enough cocaine for her to party with her friends while he "worked," Sandy was doing fine.

Many people who buy and use drugs, even drug dealers, can fly under the radar and never tangle with the law. Not so for Sandy. Her latest boyfriend was a drug kingpin who wore silk suits, drove a Rolls-Royce, and had tons of money. There were times Sandy had to take a backseat to a drug deal, but as long as this guy continued to buy her clothes and jewelry and put her up in high-class resorts with enough cocaine for her to party with her friends while he "worked," Sandy was doing fine.

Fine until the day the feds came into her workplace, asked her about the boyfriend, and kept telling her she was in a lot of trouble. When she asked them if she needed a lawyer, their response was "We don't know. Do you?" Sandy did not want to discuss any of this with her parents, so she got a friend to recommend a lawyer. The only problem was this lawyer specialized in divorces and had no experience in the area of drugs or how to defend Sandy against the federal government. She realized that she had to tell her mom and dad, and they hired a high-powered attorney to defend her. Sandy was only twenty-one at the time, and this was a huge case. She was the person the feds needed to bring the others down, and she was scared. Her thought was "Who is going to kill me?" There were eighty-seven people indicted in this case, and Sandy was one of the luckier ones. Her boyfriend was sentenced to thirty-five years to life, and most of the others received prison sentences of four years or more. Because she made a plea bargain, Sandy got three years probation for possession of cocaine.

Probation means dropping off urine samples and going to meetings on a regular basis. This was a federal program, and Sandy says, "I'm twenty-one and blond and wearing white pumps, and all the other women were black and toothless, and I saw nothing in common. We had to sit in a circle, and I did for one and a half years. I can remember thinking that I am *not* this!" Sandy stayed sober out of fear. She did drink a bit toward the end of her probation, but as long as she was passing all the urine testing, she felt she was home free. And, without the drugs and alcohol, Sandy says her life got better. Imagine that!

Sandy was working during this probation period and saved enough money to buy a house. About a year and a half into probation, her probation officer was so impressed with her progress that she called Sandy the "Star." Sandy was so perfect, she was released from probation early. She had only served half of her sentence. Today Sandy smiles at this because in her mind she wasn't going to be anything less than perfect at anything she did, and so why should probation be any different? The thought that went through Sandy's mind was that if she didn't do coke, everything would be okay. She was off probation, was working, owned her own home, and had a good relationship with her new live-in boyfriend.

Then she began to gain weight, and she recalled the same weight issue after she had quit gymnastics years earlier. How can you keep the weight off? Cocaine. She began drinking more and realized that she hated the depressive effect of alcohol. The only way she could tolerate it was to snort coke as well. It had worked before and would work for her again.

She began hiding cocaine from her boyfriend, but he found it. He was the clear-eyed adult child of an alcoholic, and so he told her that if he ever found coke on her again, he would leave. As Sandy says, "Well, he did, and he did." Her life didn't have to change because of him, and so it didn't. Sandy went on through the next six years of her life moving various boyfriends in with her because she needed their money to pay part of her mortgage and to party. She continued to be successful in her career. Sandy says she always had assistants at work, and she showed them how to do hair and how not to show up on time. Sandy was a coke addict once again.

"Maybe I need help," Sandy thought. Her goal was not to quit drugs or alcohol: It was to learn how to control them. She went to an outpatient facility, and when they asked her how much money she spent in one week on cocaine, she told them $300. She was playing down her problem because really she spent $500. This was how it worked, though: They wanted $300 a week from her for treatment. She signed up and went for about six months. She quit coke but still drank. In her mind, her problem never was alcohol. She was not an alcoholic. It was always about cocaine.

After all this time and thousands of dollars, her treatment ended with a family night. She invited her mom, and after some begging, she

"Here I was, feeling like I was doing the right thing, and I thought her support would help and she would understand."

came. Sandy isn't sure why she came at all since her mom had always been the "queen of denial." "It didn't feel supportive," Sandy says. "Here I was, feeling like I was doing the right thing, and I thought her support would help and she would understand." But Sandy says ultimately all she learned was that her drug and alcohol use was bad for her health. She saw the 12 Steps on the wall but does not recall anyone telling her to get a sponsor. They gave her the official 12-Step books, but she never read them. The only thing that came out of her time as an outpatient was reading one of the 12 Steps and knowing she had to make amends. Today she understands that she didn't exactly do it the right way, but nonetheless, she did tell her mom and dad she was sorry for everything she had done.

That's when the beginning of the end started to happen. Anyone reading this story might believe that Sandy had hit a sufficient number of bottoms, but not yet. She describes the following as her "real" bottom.

It was her mom's birthday, and there was a party for her at a country club. Sandy had disappeared for about three days prior to this event. Her boyfriend of seven years, who was living with her, did not know where she was. The day of the party, Sandy came home high and drunk, and an argument ensued. Her boyfriend drove himself to the party, and Sandy showed up later. Sandy describes her condition as being "in and out of a blackout."

Sandy remembers being in the parking lot at the end of the night screaming so loudly she woke herself out of the blackout.

All she could think of was "If I just don't do coke for three hours before dinner, I'll be able to eat, and I'll be normal." She had no clue how much alcohol she had already consumed.

She began bossing the waiter around, and her mom finally called her into the bathroom. Sandy started cursing at her mom. She remembers being in the parking lot at the end of the night screaming so loudly she woke herself out of the blackout. Her parents were driving away, her boyfriend was driving away, and at that very moment, "I swear there wasn't a soul, car, or anything on the planet, but me standing there. I looked up at the sky and for the first time in my life asked God what my life had come to. At that moment I knew I couldn't do it anymore. I really needed to get help."

God might have been ready to hear, but Sandy wasn't totally sure about giving it all up. There was still some partying left, but at least she was beginning to think about rehab. She went to see a girlfriend (a coke dealer), and together they looked up rehab facilities. They "looked." Within this period of time, Sandy also had her first experience of being fired from a job. She usually quit before getting fired, but time was not on her side. Now humiliated and without a job, Sandy describes things as "dark and lonely and crumbling mentally and emotionally."

For three weeks after her decision to find a rehab program, Sandy partied hard. So hard, in fact, her boyfriend wondered if she would make it out alive. Sandy approached a drug-addict friend who had gotten sober and asked him how he did it. He told her where he went, and her response was "I did that years ago, and it didn't work for me." He said a lot of his clients (he was a hair stylist as well) with money went to a classier type of rehab. Sandy rather liked this idea and knew she needed to go away. She had tried outpatient and probation. These, she recalls, were temporary fixes for a permanent problem. Sandy says, "I needed to be institutionalized."

"I needed to be institutionalized."

She called her mom and asked her to get money out of her house so that she could pay for treatment. Her mom told her to just go, and they would worry about the money later. Sandy made the appointment. The day came, and she was supposed to be there by 1:00 p.m. At 11:00 a.m. she called and told them she was "loaded" and couldn't come. They asked her what she had had to drink that day. The menu was a twelve-pack of Smirnoff Ice, a fifth of vodka, a pint of eighty-proof whiskey, and, oh yeah, a bit of cocaine. Sandy asked if she could come in a couple of days, and they answered yes. The day she was going to treatment, she bought two very expensive bottles of wine to pack for her "very expensive thirty-day vacation." She drank half of one of the bottles and did a half gram of coke. She didn't finish the rest.

Sandy made it to treatment and was put into detox for a number of days. She didn't even know she was in detox. All she remembers is that she did everything she was told. Later it was suggested she try a sober-living facility but one out of state. At first Sandy said no, but as time went by, she agreed and was anxious enough to call the facility every single day to make sure her bed was secure. This time her parents and boyfriend came to family weekend and in the process learned about their part in the disease. None of them, though, ever went to a 12-Step meeting or did anything at all to help themselves or support Sandy. Sandy's dad offered to send her fifty-one-year-old boyfriend to rehab for his marijuana addiction, but he refused.

Sandy lived in the halfway house for ninety days. She had a job but was uncomfortable leaving. She had always had men take care of her. Once she was able to pay her own bills, she knew it would be okay to move out. She got a roommate and lived with her for almost two years. Sandy sold her old house and made enough money to buy a new one in the new state. Today, Sandy is self-employed and, at the time of this writing, has been sober for four and a half years.

For Sandy to maintain her sobriety (which includes for her love addiction), she attends 12-Step meetings and sponsors a number of women. She has met with a number of psychologists over the years to try to figure out her childhood trauma. Sandy says that her ego is in check and that she is learning how to have healthy relationships with men. She is very much at peace today. She has reclaimed her life through her 12-Step recovery program. Sandy is only forty years old. Her new boyfriend (who doesn't drink or drug) is fifty-one. "I still like them a little older," Sandy says.

Michael

If you really want to hear about it, the first thing you'll probably want to know is where I was born, and what my lousy childhood was like . . . but I don't feel like going into it, if you want to know the truth . . . I'm not going to tell you my whole goddam autobiography or anything. I'll just tell you about this madman stuff that happened to me before I got pretty run-down.
    —J. D. Salinger, *The Catcher in the Rye*

I was fourteen years old when I took my first drink and, like so many other alcoholics I've come into contact with, loved the effect. I'd hidden a two-liter bottle of cider in my hold all for a dry "no alcohol on board" bus trip to London to watch my football team play in the 1981 centenary FA Cup final. It's now years later, and at forty-three years old, I am barely a few months sober. Manchester City was the only, obvious choice of football team for me, having been born in Northeast Manchester, and I'd followed them from the age of eleven.

My second drink, at sixteen, was while I was on a family holiday in Majorca. We were on an excursion to a "celebration," and the bus driver had forewarned all to be careful with alcohol consumption as it was notoriously, potently strong. I hadn't listened and was sick all the way home, drifting in and out of consciousness. I recall my mum and dad being particularly upset. Apparently my Dad slept with me all night. In the morning I had to thank several people who'd assisted us on our return to the hotel. I couldn't remember these people. I loved my mum and dad.

Drinking continued to be a nightmare, although I didn't really believe alcohol to be the root of the problem. My father died, and it was at this point in time that I believe I came to heavily rely upon alcohol. In reality I'd relied on alcohol since that first drink and even at such a young age knew that once I was legally permitted, pubs and drink would be waiting for me.

My mum, for all the love and support she shared with her three children—that's me and my two sisters—had always drank for as far back as I could remember. When my dad passed on, I saw a part of her die. I guess that's the way it is for many couples who've been together for an eternity. She seemed lost, and I took it upon myself to guide her through as best I could.

"I started to take miniature drinks into work to help me through. I had drink on my mind and in my throat, and I wanted more."

I had a well-paying job, organizing shipments of oil from here to there, and enjoyed work. At lunchtimes, I would drive like a lunatic and make sure that I sat down and ate with my recently bereaved mum. We'd sometimes sit in the garden and drink wine. I only had a forty-five-minute lunch break, but that was long enough to eat, drink, and reminisce. I'd get back to work and would long for the "bell to sound." I started to take miniature drinks into work to help me through. I had drink on my mind and in my throat, and I wanted more. My work was beginning to decline as my drinking increased. I arranged shipments of oil from a company in America for an unintended destination. I made another financial error resulting in a deficit of £2.5 million. My boss wasn't happy; I was desperate. We agreed that I take time off indefinitely to recuperate.

I spent the next twelve months drinking—all at the expense of the company who'd agreed to keep paying me for at least the next twelve months while I recovered.

I wasn't to return to my place of work. Furthermore, as I believed I was mentally unwell, I didn't see the harm in continuing drinking. I still didn't believe drink to be the problem.

I saw the first of many psychiatrists. One told me that for him to assess me properly, I had to go to his office on a regular basis and abstain from alcohol for nine months. That would be easy. I believed all along that I could give up at any time. I was in control. As the sessions came to a close, there was more "good news" as my psychiatrist confirmed that I had bipolar disorder. I took the "heavy-duty" bipolar-related medication as prescribed and continued to drink.

For most normal people I guess "rock bottoms" are enough to indicate that all is not well and signal time for a change. I still didn't believe alcohol to be the problem and now had my mental illness as proof and justification. During the next few years, it became increasingly clear that the medication and alcohol were not chemically compatible. I subsequently became a threat to myself and was finally hospitalized. I was assessed following a brief period of observation, discharged from the hospital, and continued to drink.

In the four years after that, drinking got worse. People would tell me that I looked fine. I would ask them time and again, "Do I look all right, am I walking straight, and is my speech coherent?" You see, physically I was all right, but my mind was breaking. I'd develop self-induced psychosis every time I drank, and every time I drank, I wanted to die. There were vain attempts at suicide—and at other times not-so-vain attempts. I was a mess, and my life was a mess.

My wife left with our daughter, and it killed me. I slept in the park, as I couldn't bear the thought of returning to an empty home. She would return only to see me pick up drinking again. Then she'd leave again. I would stay at my mum's home during these periods, and she would gladly give me alcohol. I went to bed with wine and woke up with wine. I don't blame her for my alcoholism. I hit several rock bottoms during this period. I was on first-name terms with the GMP (Greater Manchester Police), and court appearances became more of a regular feature. I was drinking around the clock and didn't know how to stop. I'd endured four stays on the mental health unit and attended detox sessions and support services. No mention was ever made of a 12-Step recovery program.

I'd always believed I could stop drinking but was now hiding drinks all over the place, so well at times that I couldn't find them. I would leave home for my mum's address and plant drinks on route just in case I was turned away. I hid small bottles in my pants, as I knew I wouldn't be frisked there. I believed for the first time that I was drinking against my will. I was beginning to acknowledge the fact that drinking could be the problem.

I went to watch Manchester City play Portsmouth at Eastlands, the home of Manchester City Football Club. I'd drunk significantly before the game and then slept during the first half. I didn't know the score but still headed for the bar at half time. In the second half I woke up, crying one minute, screaming the next. I left the stadium at full time and didn't know which way to turn. I prayed for help, something I've since heard a lot of people share, and that night I attended my first 12-Step recovery meeting. I was "off my face" and couldn't remember much about the meeting, but I definitely heard "keep coming back" and I definitely sensed hope.

I carried on drinking for another year or more and during this period was threatened with imprisonment and banned from Eastlands. Following further visits to my general practitioner, I decided to stop drinking. My GP had warned me about my liver, and I'd told him about my state of mind. We both agreed that alcohol was the problem. My first stint at sobriety lasted five months. It was almost as hard as drinking. This pattern of attempts at sobriety continued. I was in and out of 12-Step recovery, in and out of drinking, and failed to find a responsible sponsor. Of course, I look at my part in that. I endured several painful periods of sobriety.

I believed I had reached my rock bottom.

I'd only started to drink on Sunday morning, and by Sunday afternoon, I was away. The music was loud, and I was very loud. I'd not realized that my eight-year-old daughter was watching me. I carried on drinking, slipping yet again into psychotic madness, and wondering if my daughter might be impressed with the "madman" she was now witnessing in full flight. I drank for a week. I went to the hospital, and they refused to check

> "I drank for a week. I went to the hospital, and they refused to check me in. I ran to the police station, begging for help, and they drove me home in the back of a van."

me in. I ran to the police station, begging for help, and they drove me home in the back of a van. At this point in time, I have to say that the GMP were quite fantastic in each and every way they dealt with me. I am very grateful to them.

My final act was to frantically search the Internet for hope, the same hope I'd found at my first 12-Step recovery meeting yet somehow lost. I came across a website as I searched "12-Step recovery program." I knew that I could get sober. I sensed that I had to attend regular meetings but didn't want to, and I knew enough about sobriety to understand that it wasn't just about getting sober: I'd done that; I just couldn't keep sober.

I knew nothing about Kathy L., and she knew nothing about me. If I approached Kathy, she would probably just hit me with the old clichés anyway and tell me to go to recovery meetings in Manchester, but it had to be worth a go.

I couldn't have been more wrong. Kathy promised to help me, and help me she did. I believe that God brought us together. Today I am three months sober. Of equal, if not greater, significance is that we are working through the steps. I understand from Kathy that we live the steps. Of equal importance is that today there are lots of things that I don't do. In practical terms, my life is beginning to take shape. I understand that I am now working some kind of program. I even pray, for God's sake.

I am eternally grateful to Kathy for intervening in my life and undoubtedly saving it. I still cannot get over the amount of time and effort Kathy has put into keeping me sober, one day at a time. I genuinely never met anybody quite like her and probably never will. I am grateful to my wife, Sarah, for standing by me, and I am grateful to my daughter, just because . . .

That's all I'm going to tell about. . . .
I mean how do you know what you're going to do
until you do *it? The answer is, you don't!*
         —J. D. Salinger, *The Catcher in the Rye*

Katherine

The wise man in the storm prays to God, not for safety
from danger, but for deliverance from fear. It is the storm
within that endangers him, not the storm without.
         —Ralph Waldo Emerson

Most of us know that there is a genetic component to alcohol addiction. Of course, what we don't know is why it affects certain people in a family and not others. The difficult part to understand is why a young adult would turn to alcohol after watching a parent suffer from the disease. It happens, and it happens often. This is one of those stories.

Katherine remembers her mom being taken to the hospital in an ambulance and hearing her calling out for her dad. Her dad at the time was trying to comfort Katherine, who was in another room covering her ears with her hands and screaming. At this young age, she had no idea of what was going on—only that her mom was being taken away.

When there is serious addiction in a family, it is not unusual for these types of things to be shrouded in silence.

How devastating for a young child! It wasn't until later that Katherine realized the whole situation revolved around alcohol. When there is serious addiction in a family, it is not unusual for these types of things to be shrouded in silence. It is also not unusual for young children to believe their home life is normal. As they get older and begin to socialize a bit more, they realize that, perhaps, something is just not right. Katherine was in high school when she reached the point where she was embarrassed of her mom and never wanted to have friends over or even have anyone come pick her up at her house.

When Katherine was fifteen, she had permitted a date to pick her up at home. As he talked to her dad, her mom fell down the stairs right in front of them. Katherine had to think quickly in terms of choosing whether to see if her mom was okay or to run. She took her boyfriend's hand and ran. From that day on, if her dad was home to cover things, Katherine tried not to be. The problem was her dad traveled quite a bit, and no matter what, she knew her mother couldn't be left alone. In spite of her embarrassment, she did love her.

When her dad was away, Katherine became responsible for her little brother and her mom. She often would go into her mom's bedroom just to check and see if she was breathing or to calm her down if she was having a bad night and crying. She did that a lot. Crying, that is. Sometimes she would cry all night and one time tried to cut her wrists. Katherine thinks she also took some type of pills from time to time.

By the time Katherine was twenty-two, her mom was drunk every day, all day long, and crying, yelling, and swearing. She was always upset and hated everything. There were rare times when her mom was somewhat sober and content and Katherine could actually have some kind of a conversation with her. But these times were always short-lived. An hour later she would be back to her old drunken self.

No one should have to worry about another person the way Katherine worried about her mom. It was a full-time job day and night. Katherine seemed to be the only person who could ever calm her down, and she was afraid to go anywhere out of fear something would happen if her mom were left alone.

When her dad was home, he would keep watch, but if he decided to drink himself, it was even worse. They would fight, and it would get violent. Katherine described this as "like living in a dark cave with no way out." She cried herself to sleep almost every night. Even worse was the fact that she had moved on from being an embarrassed teenager to an embarrassed young adult and had no one to talk to because she was sure no one would understand.

> "The hard part was not being able to figure out how to help her and not being able to fathom why she didn't want to stop and make her life better."

In spite of it all, Katherine considered her mother one of her best friends. The hard part was not being able to figure out how to help her or get her to stop drinking and not being able to even fathom why she didn't want to stop and make her life better.

The day that saved the family finally came. No one could have imagined that a situation this horrific would be what was necessary for this broken group of people to take back their lives.

There was a swimming pool in the backyard, but it had been closed up for a few years. Katherine and her dad had been afraid that her mom would fall or jump in. When they finally opened it up again, the inevitable happened. Katherine's mom jumped in to end it all. Katherine found her. She jumped in after her and lifted her out. Katherine says, "She was so tiny and thin it was easy for me, and I'm not strong. Her skin had begun to go yellow, and the life was leaving her eyes." From this point on, it seemed like her body was going to give in any day, and Katherine would check her breathing, all the time preparing herself for the worst.

Her dad couldn't take it any longer. He cried to Katherine that he needed to get help because he couldn't handle this on his own—not for one more day. They found a counselor, and after a few sessions on his own, he invited Katherine to go with him. Katherine says that all she did was cry the entire time. The counselor told them what they already knew, "She needs to decide on her own to recover." In Katherine's mind, nothing changed. They had tried to get her sober, and she just didn't want to—or at least not at this time. "She loved alcohol more than us and herself," says Katherine. "We were looking for someone to come and take her away and lock her up. That seemed to be our only choice."

"She loved alcohol more than us and herself."

No one will ever know how it happened, but one day her dad got her mom to go see the counselor. Once there, she walked out but then walked back in, and they decided on a date for her to go into detox and also a rehab. It seemed too good to be true, but it happened—just like that!

Katherine and her dad dropped her off at detox and after she went in stood crying in the parking lot. She went on to a women's recovery home, and they visited her every weekend. It was suggested she stay for sixteen weeks, and she did. This was surely a miracle!

Before she returned home, the family fixed up the house but didn't touch the room that she used to call her "drinking room." They did, however, look for any alcohol hidden throughout the house to get rid of it. When she came home, she cleared out more of the alcohol she had tucked away but this time dumped it out in the sink.

Katherine says she couldn't have been happier to have her mother back. She is so incredibly proud of her and her years of sobriety. "She's better than ever," Katherine exclaims. "She's the best mom in the world, and she's strong, smart, and caring. She has so much love and is loved by so many people." A miracle for sure!

Katherine may not have wanted anything to do with her mom, but she wanted plenty to do with her alcohol.

But we're not done yet. Remember when Katherine was in high school and wanted nothing to do with her mom? Well, she may not have wanted anything to do with her mom, but she wanted plenty to do with her alcohol. Katherine would steal it and party with her friends. But Katherine still described herself as a "pretty good kid and finished high school and college."

Katherine ended up being a bartender for about six years. A couple of years ago, she was out at a pub with friends and some customers of hers, and they were buying her drinks. Katherine admits to drinking regularly after work but also did not make a habit of getting drunk and driving.

That night, though, a few of the friends asked her for a lift home. They got into the car, and after driving about two blocks, Katherine ran directly into a pole. Her friends were seriously injured, and one could have died. Katherine was also badly injured but was taken to the hospital in handcuffs.

She was too scared to call her parents. She waited until morning to let them know, and then when she did call, her mom answered. Her mom had worked so hard on her own recovery, and now this! Katherine had experienced how alcohol can wreck lives; she knew it firsthand. She knew how dangerous it could be and calls this the "stupidest, worst thing" she had ever done in her life.

Her mom was incredibly supportive and took care of her while she was recovering from her injuries. She took her to all her court appearances and even to the police station for fingerprints. They could even joke about it! Her mom's support was more than amazing!

Katherine had to go to jail for thirteen weeks and then do community service. Her friends recovered and are now doing okay. She is being sued by the one who almost died, but they are still friends, Katherine tells me, and she understands why her friend had to do it.

Today, Katherine barely takes a drink. She has an amazing husband and a six-month-old child. And she and her mom have never been closer. They truly are best friends!

Alice

Just as others have been caught in suffering, so have we. If we look honestly at our life, we can see the sorrows and pain that have led to our own wrongdoing. In this we can finally extend forgiveness to ourselves; we can hold the pain we have caused in compassion. Without such mercy, we will live our own life in exile.

—Jack Kornfield

When I hear the name "Alice," I always think of *Alice in Wonderland*. I loved these animated Disney films (and still do), and I remember her falling down the rabbit hole and having adventure after adventure, none of which made any sense. She got big, she got little, had a mad queen after her, and never seemed to know where she was going. She didn't know how to get home.

That's not unlike the Alice in this story. When you look at all the "adventures" in her life, you will see that she, too, had no idea where she was going, and when you might think she had finally had enough, the story starts all over again. The good news: She finds her way home in the end.

Alice is thirty-seven years old and is an alcoholic, a drug addict, and suffers from an eating disorder. Her parents divorced when she was two years old, but her mom remarried when she was four. Her grandmother and mother are alcoholics and got sober when Alice was four and fifteen, respectively. Her stepfather was extremely strict, which led Alice to learn how to manipulate people at a young age. If she did well, there was praise, but if she didn't ... well, it was bad.

Mom suffered from eating disorders, so there were quite a few "food rules" in the house. The eating disorder was the first of Alice's addictions. It began at twelve. She knows today that she was anorexic. She also knows today that this probably had something to do with the fact that she was sexually abused when she was nine but kept it a secret until she was about fifteen.

Alice describes her life then as a chest of drawers. Everything had a compartment because she felt so disorganized on the outside. If she were upset about something, her mom would send her to her room until she came out "happy." She had no choice but to stuff her emotions into the drawers because she was not permitted to express them. This is why she did not tell her mother about the sexual abuse at first. When she did, she was thrown into therapy, but her mom wanted to know all the details. End of therapy!

She took her first drink at the age of fourteen. Any fear Alice had disappeared when she drank. She felt great; she felt happy. On a normal day, however, she would binge, purge, and take laxatives to eliminate the fears she felt inside. It wasn't something that would have been noticed because Alice had a bathroom of her own. And back when Alice was ten, her mother and stepfather also had a son who started getting all the attention, which kept Alice and her activities out of the spotlight.

> *On a normal day, she would binge, purge, and take laxatives to eliminate the fears she felt inside.*

Alice believes her mom was instrumental in fueling her eating disorder. As she speaks of this, she says that she didn't think she had sugar until she was about eight and remembers distinctly an incident that occurred a bit later. There was some type of sugary cereal in the house, and she really wanted some. Her mother told her she could have some as a snack after school. When Alice got home that day and reached for the cereal, all she found was an empty box. Her mother had eaten all of it while she was at school. So when Alice had the opportunity to purchase food herself, she would eat it all and purge. She clearly remembers fund-raisers at school. She always "sold" the most candy: She ate it all and purged.

She also remembers going to a 12-Step meeting with her mom when she was a sophomore in high school. She did not have any clear memory of her mother drinking but made a promise to herself to never be like her mom; being like her would mean she was weak.

As a senior in high school, Alice went to a party given by some college kids she knew and met Sam, who would later be her husband. Alice was a pretty good kid and student. She went to a small Christian high school and was very careful to do everything expected of her because this was the type of school that would kick you out if you didn't behave. She had three months left there. She wasn't drinking at the time (actually, she had not been a "drinker" at all) and every thought shifted toward Sam. She knew that very night that she was going to marry him. She went on to community college, and they dated, but he gave her space.

Once in college, Alice did begin to drink. Today, she knows that her drinking behaviors would be classified as "alcoholic." When she drank, she felt great. On one drinking occasion, she felt totally out of herself due to the fact that someone had given her a cigarette laced with something. Her partying days had just begun, but the big moment was yet to come!

That night she drank and drank and drank. Then she was raped.

On a Labor Day weekend, there was a party that involved students from the community college that Alice attended and the major university close by. She knew a number of the football players because she had been a cheerleader in high school. That night she drank and drank and drank. Then she was raped.

Before the party began, Alice had told her friends that if they got separated, to put her car keys underneath the seat of the car. The days of cell phones had not arrived, and so once Alice was taken to the garage apartment by her assailant, she could not get in touch with her friends, or they with her. He was a big guy, a student at a university a bit farther away. He was powerful, and Alice says she was so drunk there was no way she could have moved. Her friends were pounding on the door at one point, but he held her down and covered her mouth. Once the party was over, no one checked again to see if Alice was there. He held her all night. All Alice could do was pray, "Please, God, don't let me die. Don't let me end up on the side of the road somewhere."

The weird part, according to Alice, was that he kept saying how beautiful she was and what a perfect body she had and that he wanted to be her boyfriend. He told her Sam couldn't care much for her because if he had, he never would have let her come to this party. But now the really weird part! The experience was so abusive emotionally, physically, and sexually that Alice never wanted to be thin again. She felt her body had betrayed her. From that point on until many years later, Alice stopped purging. Certain eating disorders remained, but purging meant being thin, and being thin meant rape.

The experience was so abusive emotionally, physically, and sexually that Alice never wanted to be thin again.

When it was all over, he washed her down in the shower, and to this day, Alice says she cannot stomach the smell of the particular soap or shampoo he used. She felt such shame. She didn't want anyone to know and didn't tell a soul until about three years later. Early that Sunday morning, he drove her to her car. Her keys were not under the seat. Totally devastated, she called a friend, and when the friend saw her, she could only say, "Oh my God!

What happened to you?" All Alice could answer was "Oh, I passed out and woke up with all my clothes on, and I'm fine." She was scared to death to say anything. Who would believe her? Alice is pretty sure she never went to another college party again.

Alice and Sam married about a year and a half later. Alice continued to drink, always looking to feel different, and flunked out of school. Then the couple had three children in two and a half years, and during that time, Alice didn't drink. She says she was way too busy being pregnant and nursing. Having grown up in a Christian household, Alice held Bible studies at her home, went to a moms' group at her church, and overall just wanted to be Suzy Homemaker!

She finally told Sam about the rape, and they made the decision that she should go to counseling. She did, but it didn't last long. The therapist asked too many questions that, Alice felt, implied she could have stopped it and that it was all her fault. That was *not* why she went into counseling, and so she left not feeling any better at all.

When she was pregnant with their third child, Alice and Sam moved to the southern part of their state. Sam began to drink alcoholically. Alice says she would be driving their van and when she came to a stop, all the bottles would come rolling out. Sam had an alcoholic mother (as you might recall, Alice did, too). She had gotten sober a year before the couple married. Alice also had an uncle in recovery whom she knew Sam respected, and so she had him talk to her husband about a recovery program. Alice says that she knew nothing about the program, especially the idea that if you were an alcoholic you could never have a drink again. So Sam went to a few meetings, but stopped because he said he couldn't relate.

Sam stayed sober for four months. It seemed like neither one of them understood the 12-Step process.

Alice got a job at a restaurant in the evenings. Sam worked until about 4:30 p.m., and then Alice went to work. She started drinking after work with friends. She was twenty-six and thought, after a day with kids and work, she deserved it. She started smoking marijuana and tells me she doesn't really remember the first time but does know she smoked it every day for the next two years.

Alice doesn't tell me *when* she found out she was bipolar, but does it matter? She felt the mania of all that combined with the alcohol, drugs, and eating disorders was good for her because she and Sam were not getting along. He loved the bottle, and she was being supersocial, going out every night after work and feeling great because she was not getting what she needed at home. She was a young, stressed mother of three, her kids were holding her back, and her husband... well, her husband just wasn't good for her. The eating disorder behaviors set in again as did sex outside her marriage. She was searching for some sort of security, however false, and approval through drugs, alcohol, and men. Alice quit the restaurant job because she realized that maybe all this wasn't right. Surely it was the job! That was it, the job! It wasn't the drugs, the alcohol, or the men, but the job!

Alice was back to calorie counting, eating little, and working out for hours a day. Calories needed to be saved for the alcohol. When Alice saw the movie *Coyote Ugly*, she says she wanted to be one of those girls. The closest she got though was dancing on the top of a Suburban on a camping trip. But it is one of those times that Alice says she remembers vividly. "It was August 14 and the beginning of my end. I wanted to be thin. I wanted to turn every guy's head. I didn't want to be with my husband anymore. He was my problem." This was also when she was introduced to cocaine, and she decided not to try it. She knew she would become addicted even though she still thought "I'm using marijuana and drinking everyday, but I'm not addicted."

I ask Alice if Sam knew about all this. She says at one point someone was going to tell him, but she decided to tell him first. It drew no response from him. At that moment, he really didn't care. He had his own problems. He was working about eighty hours a week, and they led separate lives. When she saw him, he was drunk. He would sometimes show up for their son's baseball games. But Alice was even more convinced that he could never give her the love or attention she felt she deserved at home.

Alice continued to party every night, and one fall evening she told Sam she wanted a divorce. She said he took their wedding photo, threw it across the backyard, and said, "Pack your shit and leave!" Alice responded with "Don't. Save it [the photo] for the kids."

She did move to a different side of town and found new friends and a drug house. Unlike the stereotype, the house was not a dilapidated shack. It's was just a house where people came and went to do drugs. Now she was really going to live her life! She was going to go to cosmetology school (something she had always wanted to do), and her kids and husband didn't care anyway. It wasn't her. It was *all* of them!

At this point, Alice became a small-time dealer. She was selling marijuana and living with a guy in what she calls a "fantasy." She was convinced they would get married and she would have her tubal ligation reversed to bear his kids. She bought a gun and carried it around everywhere with her. She tried Ecstasy, which, she says, "brought me to my knees quickly." She was drinking, drugging, barely eating, working out every day, going to sex clubs, and just living in a crazy mess. She tried crystal meth. She tells me that if she had been able to get her hands on it, she is sure she never would have gotten sober. It was the most powerful drug she had taken. She liked it so much she used it before going to a parent-teacher conference!

So where were her kids all this time? The two eldest were in school, and there was a friend of her mom's who would help out. Help out? He took care of the kids, cooked, cleaned, and did the laundry. Alice would come home in the morning to spend time with her youngest. Her husband was still drinking alcoholically at the time, so the kids didn't have either parent.

Alice was in such denial and lived in such a fantasy world that she even went to visit her birth father in another state. She says she was "totally coked out." Did I mention that she had changed her mind about the cocaine? She took the boyfriend with her and told her dad how wonderful her life was going to be, how she wanted to go to cosmetology school, have this guy's kids, and even decided she was going to have a black SUV, and he, a white SUV. Alice says loudly, "*I was out of my mind!*"

For all the drugs, alcohol, and indecent behavior, Alice had never been arrested. So her MO was to get drunk, throw up, use, and party a bit, then pass out and go again. She was incredibly lucky. She carried enough drugs on her that, if stopped, she would have been thrown in jail.

She dropped by with a U-Haul and found everything she owned sitting on the curb.

What Alice didn't know was that Sam had filed for divorce. He had called her one day to get the address of the house where she was living, but she had no clue this was why. She called Sam and asked him if she could pick up a table. She dropped by with a U-Haul and found everything she owned sitting on the curb. The teacups she had collected, clothing, porcelain dolls, books—every single thing she owned. Alice still couldn't understand why he would do this to her.

She was higher than a kite, sitting on her bed with a loaded gun.

Alice had walked out on her family in October. At the end of November, she says she woke up, and it was like a light switched off. She was higher than a kite, sitting on her bed with a loaded gun. She decided to call a friend (one of her sober friends) and told herself "If she doesn't answer, I'll kill myself." The friend answered. Alice began telling her she was going to die, and her friend agreed. If she didn't get out of the place she was in and get help, she *would* die. The biggest problem Alice had was that it never occurred to her that she was an alcoholic and drug addict. She could identify with having eating disorders because there was less shame in that. She was taking Prozac, anyway and that was a prescription, so that didn't matter.

That same morning the guy she was living with asked if she wanted to smoke some weed. As she was thinking yes, she said no. She needed to call her mom. Although she had no real relationship with her mother, she did know that, as a recovering alcoholic, her mom was the only person who would really understand. She made the call, and her mom said, "I have to get you out of there and get you to treatment." A friend of Alice's worked at a treatment facility for eating disorders. But when she called her friend to help her get into this facility, her friend could only say "Alice, you have to have an eating disorder." When Alice confirmed that she did, her friend was surprised. Alice hid these things quite well.

Since Alice was on drugs, though, her friend knew she couldn't just let her walk into the center. She needed to detox or something! No one knew exactly what drugs Alice had been taking. The friend and her husband invited Alice to go to Mexico with them. He was a pastor, and they were going on a mission trip. Alice was going to go cold turkey.

When Alice's boyfriend found out she was leaving, he kept calling and calling her, begging her to stay. Alice says she remembers feeling so bad that she was abandoning him. She even says it felt worse than leaving her kids and husband. He kept telling her she was not an alcoholic and a drug addict and she wasn't "that bad." But she just wanted help.

Mexico proved to be a complete disaster. Who wants a drugged-up alcoholic going on a church trip to detox? All Alice remembers is smoking cigarettes. She smoked, smoked, smoked, and smoked some more. The difference at this point was that the people around her were praying for her. Alice believes in the power of prayer, and so somewhere inside of her, she knew it would be okay.

About a month later, Alice went home to her children and Sam. She told her friend she was ready for rehab. Her eating disorder had been her first addiction, and with the trauma from the early sexual abuse, this seemed to be the right place to start. "God wanted me to go, and it was a Christian facility, and that was important for me," Alice tells me. She didn't want to be like her mom. She didn't want to be an alcoholic or a drug addict, and so she chose to address her eating disorder first.

Once Alice got there, she didn't think she would be able to stay, but she did...for forty-seven days. She felt as if for the first time in her life, she was able to deal with the childhood trauma and the rape, and she says the therapy was amazing. There were things, however, that Alice still didn't get. She didn't get that because of her addictions she should be working a 12-Step program with a sponsor and going to meetings. Alice thought she could get all the support she needed from her church, which had a specific program to assist addicts. She did attend that program and received a one-year chip. Then she stopped calling her sponsor and stopped meeting her. Her life began to deteriorate.

Sam was drinking more than ever, and although not drinking or drugging, Alice says she was a "bipolar absolute mess." She recalls sitting in front of the TV convinced the evangelist on the screen could heal her. She thought that she didn't need to take any action at all. If she just stayed sober and prayed hard, life would be good.

Alice drank on a couple of occasions. She didn't get drunk and couldn't tell you why she was doing it. Even her husband asked, "Are you sure you want to do that?" She was two years sober now without meetings, without a sponsor, and suffering bipolarism with suicidal thoughts. She couldn't do anything. The house was a mess. One particular day she was feeling extremely upset. She wanted to feel different and was angry. Sam and the kids were standing in the kitchen with her when she picked up her pills (her bipolar meds) and downed the entire bottle! Sam called 911. Alice said, "No, don't. The house is a mess." Sam couldn't leave the kids, so Alice ran next door and asked her neighbor to take her to the ER. She did. Alice was angry, depressed, and wanted to die. She says she wanted to "show them," but she knows today it was a cry for help.

Alice was sick. She was dying on the inside. A couple of weeks after she took the pills, her mom was helping clean the house. She said, "You know, Alice, you should go to a meeting." A few days later, Alice did just that. She went to a 12-Step meeting for alcoholics. She kept going to meetings. She realized she was spiritually bankrupt and wanted a different life. She got a sponsor who took her through the steps. Alice's life began to change.

The only thing that didn't change was Sam's drinking. While she was helping a recovering friend move to another state, Sam got a DUI. It was an extreme DUI (with a blood alcohol content above 0.15), and he was facing six felony counts. As Alice was reviewing the legal documents, all she could think was this: "My husband is a wonderful man and has never once thrown anything I have ever done in my face. He has never said a word." Sam went to meetings. He got a sponsor, and he got an attorney. He lost his license for three years and had to take a bus twenty-seven miles each way to work each day. He told Alice that every day he would get on that bus, he would remember getting handcuffed in front of his kids (yes, the kids were in the car when he was arrested).

Today Alice describes their marriage as great. She has intense gratitude to God since "because of Him, I didn't die. I feel like have gone from the pit of hell to the palace of light. I feel so blessed and I don't live in darkness anymore." Both Alice and Sam work a 12-Step program of recovery. She laughs and says, "Yeah, we're the poster kids!"

Maureen

The first thing in the human personality that dissolves in
alcohol is dignity.

—Author unknown

Maureen is a very quiet, unpretentious woman of fifty. Maureen is also an alcoholic who has been divorced three times and has two adult children. She is not a newcomer to recovery, as she has been sober for fifteen years.

Her story begins, as so many do, with family members suffering from alcoholism or other addictions. Like many who struggle with addictions, Maureen never felt comfortable with herself. She didn't feel she fit in and called herself "antisocial" and an "outsider." She had horses, and so her life revolved around them. It isn't surprising, then, that when she took her first drink at fifteen, she was primed to be a heavy drinker, maybe an alcoholic!

Being underage, Maureen and her few friends had found someone to purchase alcohol for them. It happened to be Southern Comfort, but they didn't really care what it was. They drank, and Maureen says she loved it. "I will probably remember that warm, fuzzy feeling forever," she tells me. Maureen had found the ideal way to escape from the world and specifically her parents.

When she discovered alcohol, she no longer had to physically run. She could run away without running away.

Even before she began drinking, Maureen would run away from home. She began running away at eleven years old. She wasn't happy with her life already. Maureen says,

"I was miserable and didn't know what to do to fix it. I just knew I wanted to be away." So when she discovered alcohol, she no longer had to physically run. She could run away without running away. Maureen says that she never had a "first drink"; it was a "first drunk." Things progressed from there.

My question to Maureen is "What about your parents? Did they care that you kept running away? What were they like that you would be so unhappy as a child?" Maureen says that her parents were emotionally unavailable and very rigid and controlling. Her father was particularly image-conscious, and if he heard something about another young person, his response would be "my daughter won't/ wouldn't do that!" He was quite judgmental. Maureen had a friend who had long hair, and even though he was an honor student, her father called him a "hippie" because of that hair. If Maureen got straight As on her report card, nothing was said, but if she got a B, she would be in trouble. All and all, Maureen says she grew up in a very negative environment—with no hugging or touching. There wasn't even casual relaxation in the house. So Maureen isolated herself. It was safe. Maureen learned to read at a very young age and would take her books and go into her closet with them to escape. She didn't feel loved and certainly never heard anyone say "I love you."

Surprisingly, when Maureen was nine, her parents let her have a horse, and that gave her companionship and something to do. (She did use her horse, every now and then, to run away, though.) But at the age of sixteen, she had an accident. Her hand was crushed, and her parents were afraid of infection, so after about six months, they sold the horse. Maureen was totally devastated. The only thing she had loved was being taken away from her, and so all she had left to make her feel anything at all was alcohol. All Maureen wanted to do was drink, and that is just what she did—anywhere and with anyone. She dropped out of high school. Every morning she would get in her car and say she was going to school but, of course, she didn't. She was on her way to get something to drink. It was almost two months before her parents knew she had quit school.

Maureen says her parents had to know she was drinking, and drinking every day, but they must have been in complete denial. She would come home and wouldn't be able to get out of the car, and when she did open the car door, the booze bottles would come crashing out. They knew it. She had a part-time job, and at times she would be so drunk she could not get to work, so her mom would go with her and help her with the job. Maureen says that she is sure she was a "trial and tribulation to both of them," but her dad still had this "not my daughter" mantra.

Siblings can be very different, and this was the case with Maureen and her younger sister. That sister escaped through TV. Even if she were with Maureen, her sister didn't drink. She knew what was going on, though. She knew Maureen would slip out the bedroom window and party after first coming home at the appropriate time.

Maureen did nothing but drink. She was no longer in school, and so she decided to join the military. What a disaster! She ended up being served with an honorable discharge after six weeks for "emotional reasons." Maureen said she just couldn't handle it, but the real reason was alcohol.

When she came back, she talked her parents into sending her to a boarding school. She could complete two years in one and graduate on schedule. One thing Maureen had was a brain, and she could use it. So she went to this private boarding school and threw herself into studying in order to get her diploma. There was little alcohol around, but this was okay for the short term. She wouldn't be there forever.

Sure enough, as soon as Maureen graduated, the drinking began again. She bounced from college to college. Maureen was very good at running away, and so when things became uncomfortable for her at one school, she would transfer to another. No matter where she went, she found the kids who drank just like she did. She went from one end of the country to another, but no matter where she went, it was the same. She drank until the bars closed, went home with anyone who would take her, and had a hangover the next day, only to do it again the next evening. Kind of looks like insanity, doesn't it?

There was one guy in one of her classes who used to wait for her every day, and she found it highly annoying. He wanted to chat and was keeping her from the bar. Finally she got fed up and said, "If you want to talk to me, you are going to have to go to the bar." He did. "We continued to talk and drink, and I married him."

Whoops! Maureen tells me she "forgot" that this wasn't her first marriage. This was her second. Her first happened between high school and college. She was married for seven months. It was one long drunk, and she says she doesn't remember most of it. All she remembers is that she *was* married. He was a bit older than she was, and it was an escape. It got her away from home. They did a Hollywood elopement. She snuck into the house, got some clothes, and they loaded them into the car and headed cross-country! No thoughts of anything at all. She'd known him for a week, maybe two. Her parents disowned her for a period of time and told relatives never to mention her name. She was cut off and gone!

But back to marriage number two, which she says was not made in heaven but gave her two beautiful children. They both dropped out of college, and Maureen got pregnant not even a year after they wed. They lived on a ranch. The couple had studied agriculture together, and so they both wanted to do some type of work with animals. She continued drinking and was scared half to death when she found out she was pregnant. She had been drinking hard liquor and quite a bit every day. She had a niece who had fetal alcohol syndrome, and all she could think of was that this could happen to her. She got down on her knees and asked God to please take it away—the alcohol, that is.

Maureen was terrified the entire pregnancy, which today we know is not particularly healthy for mother or baby. It was also not a good pregnancy physically. She was put on complete bed rest for three months prior to delivery, which turned out to be a C-section. The good news was that God had definitely taken the alcohol from her as she had asked. The not-so-good news was that her son was not very healthy. He had a number of complications, and for a while Maureen could only feel that the alcohol must have had something to do with it. He was always on medication, had allergies, and really didn't get healthier until he started high school.

Feeling the ramifications of drinking and perhaps the possibility that her son's health was one of those, Maureen didn't drink for five years. She threw herself into being a mom and now feared alcohol because of what it could do to her. But there was something missing. She wasn't happy. There was no emotion of any kind in her life; she was "dry." Today she says that she might have had a drink every now and then in that five-year period but only a beer here and there because she has pictures to prove it. Maureen did not permit alcohol in her house, wouldn't go to a bar, and wouldn't hang out with people who drank. She didn't even permit her parents to bring alcohol into the house. Maureen says her dry period was all about fear.

She got through a second pregnancy, and this time a daughter was healthier because Maureen was healthier. When the baby was about seven months old, Maureen decided to get a job and went to work as a manager for an apartment complex. The company decided to sponsor a happy hour for its residents, and one of her job requirements was to attend those happy hours. Maureen lasted about a month. She says she would tell them she couldn't drink (she didn't say she was an alcoholic), and they would say, "So you can have one." They didn't understand. Maureen knew she couldn't have just one. Maureen says she actually knew she was an alcoholic and was never in real denial. She knew she had a problem as a "teenage alcoholic." She just couldn't admit it to anyone. She says she could joke about it, but seriously, it was a completely different story.

Since her job was now interfering with her drinking, the only thing to do was quit. She did and decided to take a part-time job because it would give her more flexibility. At that time, her husband decided to start his own business, and so Maureen was also able to help him. The alcohol was affecting Maureen emotionally, though, and her kids began to suffer for it. She was there. She fed them. She took them to school and made sure they got where they needed to go, but she was not emotionally stable for her kids. When they were home, she propped them in a corner with a book and got on to her drinking. This is how she raised them until her son was eleven and her daughter was six.

Maureen says that "alcohol was not a very good friend" to her. She couldn't make decisions about anything and spent all her money on alcohol. The marriage was going south, and Maureen drank every chance she got. She could no longer tolerate hard liquor, which had become like poison to her, but she had to have something, or else she felt her body was just going to shut down. She drank beer then, on a daily basis. If she didn't have enough to get drunk, she wouldn't drink it unless she could take it with her to the liquor store to buy more.

Maureen was very unhappy and blamed her marriage. She thought that was her problem and that leaving was the solution. Her husband was drinking alcoholically also. There was an altercation with a neighbor, and Maureen grabbed her daughter and told her son if he wanted to go with her, to get in the car. He didn't. He stayed with his dad. She and her daughter went to a friend's house. "Not even a friend, really," Maureen says, "a church acquaintance, but it was the only place to go." She had to get out. Eventually she moved into a mobile home and continued to drink and work. She had a part-time job and was going to school, which caused a problem in the marriage. Her husband didn't want her to go to school. They would argue until three or four in the morning. During this time, Maureen was seeing a counselor, not for her drinking, but because she was so depressed and suicidal. She saw a number of counselors at one agency and was upset because every time she would get comfortable with one, he would leave. "They couldn't seem to keep a counselor," Maureen tells me. She lied to them anyway. She told them what they wanted to hear.

Every addict in recovery can recognize his bottom, and Maureen says that she was lying in bed remembering that she had been separated from her husband for about one month, was miserable and hungover, and prayed the same prayer as when she was pregnant with her son: "Please, God, take it away."

She went to her next counseling appointment, and when asked how much she drank, she lied but then said, "I'm never going to drink again because I said the same prayer as I prayed five years ago and God's going to take it away." The counselor got in her face and said, "You have got to go to a meeting!" He proceeded to tell her where she could get information on 12-Step recovery and meetings. She was terrified because she would have to admit she was an alcoholic, and that was the extreme weakness: lower than the scum of the earth. "Even though I had alcoholics in my family, I couldn't admit it. It was admitting the worst possible thing wrong with me. At this point, alcohol had been my only reward. Even if it no longer worked for me, it was still the only thing I wanted."

"Sobriety has given me a life."

She went into her part-time job that day, and she knew if she did not go to a meeting, she would drink. She knew her car would automatically stop at the place where she could buy alcohol. She knew it; she could feel it. So she went to the bookstore to get information about recovery. There was this very nice lady, a wonderful, smiling, friendly soul, who must have spotted Maureen coming through the door and took her right to the books on addiction and recovery. She made sure Maureen got what she needed.

She proceeded to tell her where she could find a meeting, what time, what the building looked like, and it sounded to Maureen as if this woman would meet her there, even though that was never said.

Instead of driving to the liquor store, Maureen drove to her first meeting. It was 9 p.m. There were four guys and Maureen, and she felt scared. She sat there thinking the woman might walk through the door any second. She never came. Then the men started talking and laughing, and within fifteen minutes or so Maureen was *home!* Her thought was, "If these guys can do it, I can do it. They were happy, laughing, sharing their stories, and it took me a while to understand how anyone could have anything to laugh about, but I wanted what they had. I have been sober ever since."

Sobriety doesn't mean life is without conflict. Maureen went on to marry a third time, this time to someone in recovery. It was not a good match. Unfortunately for him and Maureen, he could not remain sober, and it reached a point where Maureen could no longer tolerate it. It ended in divorce.

Maureen went on to get a master's degree in education and is teaching on a Native American reservation. She believes her children have issues because of the environment she created when she was drinking. Her daughter is now married and lives close by, and Maureen believes she has and always did have a good relationship with her son. Her children are both sober, but any alcoholic in recovery can spot certain behaviors and be a bit concerned. Maureen sees those in her son although he has never had a drink.

"I thank God for my sobriety every day because without it, I'd be dead."

To maintain sobriety, Maureen attends not only 12-Step meetings for recovering alcoholics but also 12-Step meetings for those who are codependent. She likes variety and will go to different meetings throughout a week. "If I'm sitting at home and have nothing to do, I go to a meeting," Maureen says. Maureen believes that since she took her last drink fifteen years ago, she hasn't ever come close to picking up a drink. She prays and has found a God of her own understanding. "Sobriety has given me a life. It's not a perfect life, but I can function. I'm employable, I have a relationship with my family, and I can go places and do things. I'm not where I want to be yet, but I believe that sobriety has given me the ability to get there as long as I stay sober. It brought me back to a relationship with God, and that is what makes it all possible. I thank God for my sobriety every day because without it, I'd be dead. Yes, it has given me a life!"

Jody

Consider how hard it is to change yourself, and you'll understand what little chance you have in trying to change others.

—Jacob M. Braude

I came into a 12-Step recovery program seven years ago. That night my alcoholic/addict partner was passed out on the couch; it was Memorial Day weekend. I felt hopeless. The fantasy I had of a wonderful three days was ruined. I felt trapped and invisible; like I didn't matter. I felt like I was no longer part of the functioning world. I felt like my life could only change if he changed. And it didn't look like that was going to happen anytime soon.

The truth is that I had been involved with alcoholics/ addicts my entire life, and it occurred to me that nothing had changed for me in thirty-five years. That scared me. One day in recovery I would learn the difference between pity and love. When only one person feels pity for the other, the relationship doesn't thrive. When two people feel love for each other, all things are possible, and the sky's the limit. But I wouldn't be asking myself about that distinction until I got a sponsor and started working Step One in a recovery program.

I was not brought up in an alcoholic household. I was brought up with rage and depression. My parents did the best they could with what they had. There was tension at home, sibling rivalry, money pressures. My mom always seemed upset and disappointed. Today I understand that she was sexually abused by her father and traumatized. My dad spent a lot of time sleeping off headaches. Today, I know he was depressed. At the time, all I knew was that it always felt like something was wrong.

I lived in my head a lot as a kid. I wanted to be alone and was jealous of other kids. My feelings always felt larger than life. When the other kids were making s'mores at Girl Scout camp, I was locking one of the campers in her cabin. Today, I understand that my thinking was already distorted.

At thirteen I was immediately attracted to boys with drama: boys in trouble, boys on drugs, boys who wanted sex. I didn't have a clear thought process. The scent of drama led me to all my decisions. And of course there were the secrets I kept: the fear and shame that isolated me from my family and other kids my age. At fourteen I started working full-time after school and saved enough money to buy my first car two years later. I kept three men in my life at that time: an alcoholic high school senior, a glue-sniffing older man, and a gay heroin addict. When I wanted to give the addict my entire savings instead of buying a car, my parents intervened. So I bought the car and turned the keys over to him—the car was totaled in a week.

I couldn't wrap my brain around working for my own needs. I couldn't wrap my brain around being worthy of owning a car. I couldn't conceptualize that my time had any value if it wasn't invested in another person. I never felt like I was enough. My thinking was broken, and that brought trouble into my life.

I never admitted to my parents or the insurance company the truth about who was driving the car. I let fear and shame make up a brand-new story and a brand-new reality. I continued to live a drama-based life throughout high school. When I graduated, I hopped in my car and drove across the United States until I reached San Francisco. My distorted thinking kept me looking for trouble. I found an apartment to share and immediately met and fell in love with a speed freak twice my age. He had custody of his daughter, and that was a shame—because I was in no way mature enough to care for her. As soon as he left for work and she left for school, I left to look for trouble around town. My appetite for drama was enormous, and San Francisco in the 1970s had enough to satisfy me.

When I ran through every addict/alcoholic relationship I could find there, I moved back to New York for more drama, more married men, and more alcoholics, until I finally met my match. This was a man with substance-abuse issues, physical problems, and an emotional landscape that stirred me to my toes. We moved in together, and our life was a high-wire act. But I will never forget the day that his hands were wrapped around my throat, and I thought, "He just opened a beer." It had never occurred to me that there was always trouble when he drank. I had always thought that *I* caused the trouble. I felt completely responsible for everything. Today, of course, I understand that I *am* completely responsible—but only for my part in things. But at the time, I had no idea where I ended and where he began. Drama levels the playing field, and personal boundaries are blurred.

That relationship ended with a court order and a PO box for me. I still have that PO box almost thirty years later. It reminds me every day when I pick up my mail that I once had to hide. I was once so consumed with fear that I didn't want my address on any piece of paper. The truth is that it was never a relationship: It was a reaction-ship. We didn't relate to each other as equals. We reacted as winner/loser. That's one of the ways that I've been affected by someone else's drinking. Eat or be eaten—that's my perspective. There's always an enemy, so protect the supply. And alcoholism threatens my supply of serenity. I'm used to battling alcoholism. And although I believed in that very persistent illusion that there was a winner and a loser, the truth is that there was a loser and a loser—every time.

> "I was worthless unless I was saving someone. So I kept an apartment to house the alcoholics in my life, a job to pay for their needs, and a car to drive them around."

I'm focused on the relationships in my life because this is a disease of relationships. Our symptoms come out when we are in relationships. Our self-pity, fear, jealousy, resentment, shame, contempt, rage—it all comes out when we are involved in any way with another person. Families, coworkers, authorities, partners—relationships are trouble.

I was superficial with my parents and downright hostile toward my sister. I was angry, irritable, and unreasonable.

I always maintained an apartment, job, and car throughout the years of chaos. In hindsight, my motives were not self-care. My diseased thinking believed that I was worthless unless I was saving someone. So I kept an apartment to house the alcoholics in my life, a job to pay for their needs, and a car to drive them around. I would get paid and immediately hand the money over to my partner. I would hand them the keys to my car and then scramble to get my own rides. I would unplug my phone so that "he" could sleep. I would crouch for hours at the bottom of the stairs, waiting for "him" to wake up and then go into restaurant mode. I willingly went to any lengths to focus on the alcoholic. I thought that was love. Today I know that's called drama.

"Drama is like salt for me. Life is bland without it."

Several alcoholics later, I was in my late thirties when I met my current partner. He was an alcoholic/addict, sober when I met him, but he relapsed nine months later. I suspect I was relieved. Drama is like salt for me. Life is bland without it. We had a wild ride for twelve years—rehabs, jail, hospitals, five police cars driving up to my suburban condo at 2 a.m., locksmiths, car chases, and threats—seasoned with weeks, and once a whole year, of sobriety. But one Memorial Day weekend I woke up and was sick and tired of being sick and tired.

I called his sponsor, told him to get my partner out of the house, and he said, "Sure, but get yourself to a 12-Step meeting." I had never heard of meetings for people like myself. I looked it up in the phone book and was immediately resentful that they didn't list the denomination of the church. It would take a few years in 12-Step recovery meetings before I understood that my reaction was the only qualification I would ever need to be in program. Even if there was no active drinker in my life, the fact that I could get resentful looking up a phone number should have told me there was something wrong with me—and it wasn't the alcoholic.

Coming into recovery was painful. I had created so many airtight cases for my righteous indignation. I felt so misunderstood. I started to feel angry toward people in program. I started to feel resentful and jealous of people in program. I compared my low-bottom alcoholic to their high-bottom alcoholic. I compared my trouble to their trouble. And I finally started to understand that my life was unmanageable because of my focus.

I began to see that I was powerless over alcoholism but not helpless, powerless over the symptoms I suffered from having been affected by someone else's drinking. I came into the program looking for someone to blame for the trouble in my life. Step One showed me that it wasn't someone, but something: alcoholism.

Alcoholism has physical, emotional, and spiritual symptoms, but the cure is spiritual, spiritual, spiritual. I came to believe through Step Two that there was a Power greater than the trouble that could restore me to wholeness, restore me to reality. Powerless: Step One. But not helpless: Step Two. And in Step Three, I made

> *"Alcoholism has physical, emotional, and spiritual symptoms, but the cure is spiritual, spiritual, spiritual."*

a decision to turn my distorted thinking over to that Power. I didn't trust yet, but I did believe.

Today I continue to practice spiritual principles in all my affairs. I'm active in the program, speak with my sister every day, and am grateful for the time I spend with my parents. I've had to let go of some people in my life and let God redirect my energies. I live simply and allow others to simply live.

Chuck

We are so accustomed to disguising ourselves to others that in the end we become disguised to ourselves.
—François, Duc de La Rochefoucauld

Chuck is a sex addict and an alcoholic. He used drugs for a period of time when he was sent to Vietnam but doesn't really include drugs in defining his addiction. He tells me that his sex addiction was the stronger of the two he does suffer from but goes hand in hand with alcohol. In other words, alcohol allows the sex addiction by diminishing any moral misgivings about his sexual behaviors.

He remembers that at age eight or nine, he spent lots of time hanging around the monkey bars and swings to be around the girls and peer up their skirts. This may seem like typical little-boy behavior, but what Chuck remembers is that none of his friends were with him. They were off playing ball. As he got older, he played "doctor" with the neighborhood girls and would actually give them a quarter for it. Again, that doesn't seem terribly unusual, but today he is sure he had a much stronger interest in those sorts of things than any of his friends did.

All in all, Chuck thought he had a normal childhood until he got into therapy years later. His parents are still together after sixty-seven years of marriage, so there was a solid family unit. His mom, however, was and still is what Chuck describes as a "very sexual person." She has always been totally obsessed with her looks to the point where she got breast enhancements at the age of seventy-two! She also suffers from untreated depression, and when Chuck was young, he would be the go-to person for her whining and complaining.

Chuck's dad was away quite a bit either for his work or the Army Reserves. At first I thought that Chuck was the first son or an only child since his mom seemed to depend on him, but he did have an older brother. That brother had a very close relationship with their father, and they have maintained that closeness even today. Chuck did not have a close relationship with either his brother or his father. His brother shared their mother's perfectionism, and so having to share a room with Chuck became an obsessive issue.

Chuck felt that nothing he could do would be good enough for his dad. After talking with his dad adult-to-adult later on, Chuck discovered that his father felt that in order to encourage a child, you had to keep raising the bar. As a child, Chuck read that as never good enough. These family dynamics led Chuck to low self-esteem and a lot of negative attention at school.

At an age when most kids don't care much about religion, Chuck was different. When he was in sixth grade, his parents began taking the boys to church to expose them to religion, but as Chuck puts it, "I took to it." He took to it so much that he went to a vacation Bible school during the summer and became enamored with the woman who was holding the school in her home. He put her on a pedestal and even after that summer remained involved with church. In junior high he was the president of a local youth for Christ organization.

The reason Chuck feels this is important to his story is that the whole religion thing conjured up an incredible amount of guilt for the sexual yearnings he had. He hadn't really acted on any of them with the exception of looking at his dad's magazines when his parents were not around and "doing what young boys do." He had not started drinking at this time, and his moral compass prevented him from taking any steps toward his desires and girls. His teenage years were filled with angst.

Chuck was so sick that he lay in the street vomiting as the kids were coming home from school.

Enter alcohol and its enabling function! At fifteen and a half, Chuck and two of his buddies decided to ditch school and raid everything in his friend's dad's bar. Chuck was so sick that he lay in the street vomiting as kids were coming home from school. He doesn't know how he got home or got past the scrutiny of his parents, but he did. The next day at school he was a hero! He ditched school again and got drunk, and in the eyes of the other kids, he was so cool. And so alcohol became a friend to Chuck. It was easier to relate to others, easier to deal with his angst, and easier to get past all those teenage inhibitions, especially around girls.

It made sense that his religious convictions began to wane. He stopped going to church. He still had thoughts and feelings about religion but didn't practice them. And furthermore, the woman he had so idolized at Bible school was no longer permitted a place in the church. She was considered too radical. Chuck decided that organized religion was just another clique or cult, and that led him to pull away from the church completely. The angst, however, stayed with him because the religious ideals were not going away, but he was now drinking, which increased his sexual thoughts and desires.

He dated in high school, and it was normal, healthy dating. In his junior year, he was a football player, and he started dating a cheerleader. They were quite enamored with each other and were into the kissing and petting, but that was it. One weekend they were at her sister's house, and they were alone. She wanted to have sex. He declined. This "no" was a combination of his still-intact morals and the fact that he had not been drinking. He felt they needed to wait until marriage. Well, that never happened. She went away to college, and he stayed in his hometown for college, and within a month he got the "Dear John" letter.

His attitude toward sex was "anyplace, anytime, anyone."

This was very significant in his sexual life because his mental and emotional reaction to this was "What the hell am I saving myself for?" He promptly went out and had his first sexual experience. She was a promiscuous eighteen-year-old married woman with a new baby. From that point on, Chuck's attitude toward sex was "anyplace, anytime, anyone."

It was the Vietnam War years, and at nineteen, Chuck was drafted into the Army. He wound up enlisting instead, but still went to the Asian theater. By that time he was a heavy binge drinker. He didn't drink daily, but when it was time to bring out the booze, "I was a real party hound." He lived in a "hooch" (a ten-man tent on a wooden frame), and a few of the other guys were heavily into drugs, mostly marijuana because it was readily available. They kept trying to get Chuck to try it, but he refused. He would drink, and drink like a fish, but no drugs! After about three months, his buddy was getting ready to return home and said, "Do me a favor. Just try it [marijuana] once as a present to me as I leave." Chuck said yes. He never looked back. It was such a wonderful experience he became a daily marijuana/hash smoker as well as a drinker. The days never changed. They would get up in the morning, do their assigned tasks, get off from work, have dinner, and get loaded. This was life for nine months.

There was at least one day off a week, and that was usually on a Sunday. They would go into town to a bar, get loaded, and then slip in the back with the prostitutes. This was Chuck's introduction to prostitution as well. It was how he and a lot of other young men lived with the trauma and stress of being in a war zone. Many of these stresses have stayed with them even after many years. Chuck says that he learned one thing in Vietnam, and that was "When things got tough, the tough got drunk and stoned and, in my case, turned to sex. Sex, drugs, and alcohol!"

Chuck returned to the States when he was twenty-one and thought he would be leaving all that behind. No more war zone. No more threats. But the behavior continued because he returned when many of the other guys did, and so the partying continued. The good news for Chuck was that although the drinking and drugging continued, his sexual appetites did not. He was no longer seeking out prostitutes or any girl who would have him.

He did meet a girl when he was in the service and changing duty stations. They had a sexual relationship, and she did come to visit him once. He met another girl at the same time but did not have sex with her, because they were just friends. This girl later became his wife.

He continued to write to his future wife when he came home from Vietnam and moved to the Southwest to go to school. He asked her to come and live there but with no promise of marriage. This was the early '70s and so her parents were not happy about it. After a period of about three or four months, they were engaged, and life was good.

Two years into the marriage, Chuck was at a work-related party, so spouses weren't invited. He and another guy got very drunk and were basically having their way with one of the women (Chuck's boss, nonetheless), and she was very willing. That was Chuck's first acting-out experience while married, and he felt completely shamed by it. He felt strong remorse and vowed to himself that he would never do that again... until the next time. And the next time came about three months later, same situation, same lady, only this time, it went further. There was intercourse, and from that point on, Chuck says, "the floodgates were opened on my sex addiction." It went from any woman willing to have sex to prostitutes.

He left his chosen profession and went to work for a company that had interests in hotels and casinos in Nevada and Atlantic City. For Chuck, being in these places was like being a kid in a candy store. There were absolutely no restraints whatsoever. He was high enough in the organization to have signing authority for food, drinks, and rooms. Between free drinks and the ability to go to any one of the properties and check into a room, Chuck could either pick

"If life were fair, I'd be dead."

up girls who were young and impressionable or simply call down to the front desk and "order up a hooker."

These few years were wild and crazy. When Chuck remembers those times, he uses his favorite quote: "If life were fair, I'd be dead." The only reason Chuck feels he is alive today is that God had a different plan for him. His wife suspected that Chuck was not exactly being faithful, and she had not wanted to move in the first place. Chuck had bribed her with a new car. She spent a lot of time without him, though, because he enjoyed Tahoe more than any other place. "If Las Vegas is sin city, Tahoe is the devil's playground," he says. "It was one big party. Work during the day and party hard at night."

What Chuck didn't realize until later was that his wife was being lured to the other side as well. It turned out she was having an affair, and so both of them were heading down life's fast lane and straight for the crash and burn. The reasonable side of Chuck told him that this was not a life he wanted to lead, and he got reassigned back to the city he had lived in before.

There was now one very important thing that happened that Chuck refers to as a kind of intervention. An intervention doesn't have to mean a person has hit a bottom, but in Chuck's case, that is exactly what happened. One result from all his sexual activities was that he contracted genital herpes. It was then that he felt that if he did not change his sexual behaviors, he would die. He could not control any of his addictions. The couple decided to find a counselor for help.

Chuck tells me that this was the second time he had seen a counselor and that the first time it was actually a psychiatrist. He had wanted to talk about his sexual behaviors. He knew they were not normal, and he was feeling guilty. He needed some answers so he could know what to do. His recollection of what the doctor told him is "Well, it seems to me that you are a little oversexed, but it is kind of normal behavior and nothing to be concerned about. You'll grow out of it." Chuck also says that he is not sure if those are the exact words, but this is what he got out of it. Permission!

By the time the couple returned to their original home, they were both a mess. They both had violated their marriage vows, and they went through about two years of counseling. They had two children by then and even took the kids to a park and told them they were going to get a divorce. The kids were devastated. Chuck says that to this day, they still remember this as a very significant traumatic event in their lives. The next day, after both had thought about what they had told the kids, they decided "Let's not do this. Let's try harder." They made promises to each other and decided to do their best.

All through their counseling sessions, alcohol was never considered to be a big issue in the overall scheme things. It was never mentioned that Chuck might be an alcoholic or that he even had a drinking problem. Their counseling was focused on their relationship and extra-marital affairs and promises that they would remain faithful to each other.

Unfortunately, what was in Chuck's head and what he was saying to his wife were two different things. He was still living a dual life. He couldn't stop having sex outside the marriage; he made the promises because he loved his wife, his kids, and his family, but he did not have the power to stop. He told himself that he would just have to be absolutely extra careful. And from that point on, that is exactly what he was … extra careful. He was still drinking and now acting out sexually with many different women, including the wives of people they saw socially. There were one-night stands and longer-term affairs. His was a well-hidden double life. He was never caught.

It was the drinking that began to bother him. He hadn't come to the point where he could call himself an alcoholic for the usual reasons. He was a high-functioning binge drinker. Chuck didn't start out drinking daily but soon would have anywhere from a couple of glasses of wine to an entire bottle in one evening. Weekends were different. Drinking on weekends had no limits. His wife became concerned about his drinking, and Chuck started to believe that his acting out sexually was a direct result of drinking. If he could stop drinking, maybe he could stop the sex addiction. So he went to a 12-Step meeting for alcoholics. He sat there and related to the stories, looking for the similarities, not the differences. He looked around and saw the 12 Steps and 12 Traditions on the wall, but the whole "God" thing made him say "Not for me." As religious as Chuck had been as a young boy, the Vietnam experience had made an agnostic out of him. He felt that if there was a God, he didn't care an iota about the world and definitely not about Chuck.

For the next five years, he did not attend a meeting. He would simply stop on his own. He was actually fairly successful for about three years and felt he was correct about the link between drinking and sex. There were actually two kinds of sexual acting out according to Chuck: one was sex outside the marriage, which he did not do when he was not drinking, but the second was sex "in" the marriage, meaning adult bookstores and masturbation.

On his birthday, which happened to be December 31, he decided that it wouldn't hurt to have a glass of Champagne. He did, and nothing happened. His anniversary was at the end of May, so he figured, "If it worked for my birthday, surely I can have a drink for this occasion." He had two or three glasses of Champagne and within a week was full-blown drinking. He did, however, have the willpower not to engage in sex outside his marriage.

One rather fateful evening, Chuck was at a business meeting and had to give a speech and hand out a few awards. He was very nervous, and so he figured a glass of wine would calm him. He has no idea how much alcohol he consumed because he can only remember walking onto the stage. He was in a blackout. He left the meeting with a woman who was going to take him to a bar, but he stopped in the parking lot and propositioned her instead, and she was smart enough to ditch him. He then drove to a divorced friend's home about 12:30, banged on the door, and propositioned her until she threw him out on his ass. By the time he got home, he was still drunk, and when the alarm went off a few hours later, he felt the same. His wife rolled over and said, "Get help, or get out!"

Chuck says that this was the big intervention in his career as an addict. He was ready for help but very reticent. His company had an employee-assistance program, and later that day he met the director of an outpatient facility. This was Chuck's next intervention because he began to understand the concept of a Higher Power. Chuck says that this guy explained how all he had to do was choose something greater than himself and went on to talk about it until Chuck totally got over his concerns about 12-Step recovery.

He would love to say that he lived happily ever after, but that's not the case. He was given a battery of tests and the result was "You've got a problem other than alcohol and drugs, but we're going to focus on getting you sober first and strongly recommend you deal with your problems with sex." Chuck spent the next two years getting sober but still acting out "inside" his marriage. His sponsor happened to have strong ties to a facility that deals quite a bit with trauma and sex addiction. Chuck started to see a counselor there and began his therapy and recovery from sex addiction.

> *"Sex addiction was much more difficult than alcohol and drugs because it dealt with the very core of our existence."*

"Sex addiction was much more difficult than alcohol and drugs because it dealt with the very core of our existence," Chuck shares. He spent the next five years in intensive therapy, which included a five-week stay at what he calls "trauma camp." During the family weekend, his therapist thought he should disclose all his sexual activities to his wife. She was devastated. Her feeling was that he dumped all this stuff on her and sent her home. She had no support. Chuck's therapist convinced her to go into a facility for about a month for her depression. Chuck says this was a "visual intervention" for him. His wife had gone from a healthy 130 pounds to a frail 105 in a month, and she looked horrible. It brought up all the shame and guilt that had surrounded Chuck all his life.

For the following year, it was touch and go. They each had their own therapists, went to meetings, and did whatever they needed to do to survive emotionally. After another year, and Chuck isn't sure exactly how it happened, they both kind of decided "Look, we love each other, we do want to make it, so let's forgive each other and move on." At that point, Chuck believes they really began to heal. He tells me how much he always loved his wife. His love for her is a deep respect for her as a person and what she believes in. Today they enjoy activities together and give each other enough space to enjoy things on their own. According to Chuck, the relationship they have now is closer and stronger than it has ever been. It has been forty years!

Chuck feels blessed. He says that the road to recovery has been tough and remembers the first eight years out of thirteen as being extremely difficult. The last five have been a bit easier. He knows he is not cured or suddenly healed. He has no compulsions to drink but, like many alcoholics, might have a nostalgic feeling here and there. "Have a glass of wine...just one!" He smiles because he knows he can't touch alcohol...not a drop. He also has a nostalgic feeling about sex, mainly because at age fifty-seven he had prostate cancer and as he tells me, "had all of that stuff removed." His body knows what it can't do, but he says his head doesn't. "I still like to look at women. I still appreciate the female form. I just have to make sure that my head doesn't go off in the wrong direction."

Chuck stays very close to his recovery program. He has to share the things that come up and talk about them to his recovering friends and then let it go. He no longer has the physical ability to engage in intercourse, but he still has the ability to act sexually with a woman. "So, I'm still a danger to myself and to others. I guess I'd say that that's my story, and I'm sticking to it!"

Gia

The truth about our childhood is stored up in our body, and although we can repress it, we can never alter it. Our intellect can be deceived, our feelings manipulated, our conceptions confused, and our body tricked with medication. But someday our body will present its bill, for it is as incorruptible as a child, who still whole in spirit, will accept no compromise or excuses, and it will not stop tormenting us until we stop evading the truth.

—Alice Miller

If I asked you to talk about one of your earliest memories, what would you tell me? You might tell me about a favorite toy, your first pet, a special birthday, or maybe a memorable vacation. How many people do you know would tell you that their earliest memory is being in the garage with their dad, being taught how to make a marijuana pipe out of an empty toilet paper roll and tinfoil and being very excited to help him? I know of only one: Gia.

Gia's dad was an alcoholic but stopped drinking when Gia was in her teens. Unfortunately, a lot of damage had already been done to Gia, her mom, and her little sister. Gia remembers trying to comfort her sister as her mother dragged her drunken father down the hallway or down the stairs by the feet to lock him out of the house. Although the drinking stopped, he still smoked marijuana and does to this day. He will tell you, Gia says, that he has been sober for twenty years!

He may not have been drinking, but he would still be labeled a "dry drunk." Gia calls him a "very sexual person." He enjoyed porn, and it was embarrassing to this otherwise female family when he would ogle women in their presence. Gia knew that he cheated on her mom. It didn't make her love him less; it made her want to be perfect and have the perfect body because that is what men wanted. If she didn't take care of herself, someday someone would cheat on her.

About the time Dad stopped drinking, Gia watched a TV special about a girl who had an eating disorder (bulimia). Instead of finding it scary or repulsive, Gia thought it was brilliant—in fact, genius! "I can do this," she thought. "I can eat all this stuff and not pay the price, not have to gain weight."

Gia discovered how to binge and purge, and while she was practicing that, she began to experiment with alcohol. Drinking became a part of her young life, and acid was added soon after. The combination of alcohol and acid led to a friend's boyfriend raping Gia at a party. She was so high she could not function and until she saw a therapist years later never recognized what had been done to her. What she did know was that everyone thought she was having consensual sex with this boy, and so all she got was a reputation. Years later, Gia says, those friends who had condemned her came back and apologized.

You might think Gia would curtail the drinking after she'd gotten such a bad rap, but she didn't. Since her father had stopped drinking, there was no alcohol in her home, but all her friends' parents drank, and so raiding their liquor cabinets got to be this great secret. Gia and her friends were not even old enough to drive. She says they would do normal things like ride their bikes with this "magic tingle" inside of them. Fun was drinking and then interacting with adults who would be interacting with them as children but not knowing the kids held a secret. The secret, alcohol, made them giddy, silly, funny, and powerful!

By the time Gia was a senior in high school, she was actually over the drugs (acid and Ecstasy) but not the eating and the drinking. She was not willing to believe she had a drinking problem but was aware that she always had to drink until she vomited while her friends could just stop. Yet through this, she maintained a very high grade point average, was on the homecoming court, was a prom princess, and from the outside looked good. Gia admits that she really cleaned up her act.

She began selling her blood at the local blood bank to get the money to eat, binge, purge, drink, and buy laxatives.

College for Gia was across the country. It was a purposeful geographic move, but she didn't realize it at the time. It wasn't long before her drinking took off like a rocket; likewise she gained weight, as many college freshmen do. She was in a relationship for the first time in her life, too. Still, when she looked at herself, she says she saw the Michelin Man and said to herself, "Who the hell are you?" Gia returned to what she knew would take the weight off but added diet pills to the mix.

She began selling her blood at the local blood bank to get the money to eat, binge, purge, drink, and buy laxatives. Drinking was what everyone did, but the eating disorder was her secret.

This was Gia's life for the next few years in college, yet she was going to graduate on time and with spectacular grades. But she wasn't sure what she wanted to do, so right before graduation, she called her dad and said, "Dad,

I think I would like to teach." So her dad told her to come back home and go to graduate school there.

It might be hard to imagine that her life had been any-thing but terrible, but Gia says that things got even worse once she returned to her hometown. She started getting a lot of criticism from people about her fluctuating weight, and the eating disorder got worse. Gia says her face looked like a Cabbage Patch Kid doll from all of the purging. She was going to graduate school and bartending nights and weekends but felt like any time she had was spent alone. Because she was alone, she occupied her time by drinking and throwing up every single night.

Gia's sister was five years younger and was smart enough to see Gia had big problems. This caused a rather tumultuous relationship between the two. Her parents ignored Gia's condition and didn't say a word. Only once did her dad ever mention anything at all to Gia. Gia would throw up out her sec-ond-floor window, and Gia's dad noticed damage on the side of the house. Instead of talking to her about the problem, he said, "If you are going to throw up, throw up in the fucking toilet!" All she could say was "All right."

She used two hundred laxatives a day. It was her secret.

Gia had never told anyone about her eating disorder, but it was obvious to her that her dad knew. She feels her mom knew also but tells me that as much as she loves her mom, her mom just didn't know how to help. She felt if she ignored something, she could keep it from being real.

Feeling upset and uncomfortable at home, Gia moved out and lived on her own for the first time. As Gia says, she was now "really off to the races." She started buying hundreds of dollars of food every day, bingeing and purging, and drinking bottles of the cheapest alcohol she could find. All her money went to these as well as laxatives. She used two hundred laxatives a day. It was her secret. She couldn't even sit in a classroom because she had to spend so much time in the bathroom. It was madness.

At school one day, she noticed a flyer about a women's wellness center. She sought out a therapist, and when she told her about all her behaviors, the therapist was aghast. She immediately put together a team of professionals to help Gia. After a full medical exam and other testing, it was determined that Gia was depressed, among other things. She did tell them about her drinking, but it was her eating disorder that was the primary concern. She was spending hundreds of dollars a week on bingeing, purging, and laxatives. The nutritionist of the group was helpful, but when Gia graduated a month or two later, she quit treatment. This is also when her drinking took off.

For some reason, even though she was living alone, she had begun to hide her liquor bottles. Then she realized she had to move back home because she had no more money. She bought huge bottles of vodka and would fill up soda cans, thinking no one knew. Still her parents said nothing. That is, until one night she was drinking and dropped her glass. She was lying in bed and believes she was passed out cold. They found the bottle of vodka and took Gia to the hospital. But it wasn't just any hospital: It was a psychiatric ward with barred windows and padded doors. She kept crying and saying "I was only drunk. I'm not crazy. What are you doing?"

She still isn't sure why they didn't take her to a hospital to detox, but they did not. It was awful, and no matter how she sobbed and cried and tried to convince everyone she wasn't crazy, she now realizes that no one in a psychiatric ward thinks they are crazy. She would call her parents but to no avail. Only one doctor talked to her prior to her release and asked her how much she drank. When she told him (and she admits that like any good alcoholic she lied), he asked her if she had ever heard of a recovery program for alcoholics. She had not. When she got home, though, the first thing she did was look it up in the phone book and attended a meeting.

The meeting was in a church in her hometown, and because Gia's dad was known in the community, she felt mortified. She was twenty-two years old, sitting in a meeting with a group of alcoholics, and decided she was not one of them. She just drank a little too much, and she was sad. Yes. That was it! She stopped drinking for six months.

By that time, Gia had finished graduate school and wanted to go back to the Southwest where she had gone to college. She got online and applied for as many teaching jobs as she could. She wanted to get away from her parents but to please them at the same time.

She found a job teaching third grade and an apartment. She loved the children but was as lonely as ever. Before long, she was back to the hundreds of dollars a day for food, up to two hundred laxatives a day again, and drinking. If she didn't drink, she couldn't sleep. This cycle was horrendous, and she knew she could not possibly be putting in 100 percent at work yet won accolades for her ability, including Teacher of the Year. Today, Gia says she can't even begin to wrap her mind around how these things happened because she was such a mess.

Teaching third grade was wonderful. The kids loved her. They wanted to wear the same color nail polish she did and couldn't give her enough gifts and hugs. It wasn't enough. Gia admits to me that she actually stole their food when they were out at recess. She would take it out of their lunch boxes, and if they didn't eat all their food (and most didn't), she would go through the garbage and eat whatever they had thrown out. Then she would purge.

Gia had to wear adult diapers because of all the laxatives. She would bring them to work with her and made sure they were double bagged. One day a secretary saw through the bag and said, "Are those Depends?" Gia was mortified but came up with the excuse that she was doing a science experiment with them.

At this time, Gia's parents moved near Gia, and she did visit them occasionally. Gia says that she was as skinny as can be but her face and neck were fat and swollen, a result of her drinking and purging. She started calling in sick at work. She drank on parents' night because she "had to." She went as far as to call the school and tell them her grandmother had died. They knew she would have to fly across the country and wouldn't expect her back for a few days. Gia's plan was to just stay in her apartment and drink, eat, and purge for as long as she could.

She actually stole the kids' food when they were out at recess.

As luck would have it, while Gia was partying all alone, her father called her to tell her that her grandmother had actually died. Gia was sure that it was her fault. She had willed it by lying about it to her employer. She now had an even better reason to drink and was found unconscious in her apartment by the maintenance man who had to break down the door.

Gia was once again taken to a hospital psychiatric ward, and yet she still could only say what she had said before: "I'm not crazy. I just drank too much." Over and over, Gia would say, "I was sad." Yet everyone else was beginning to see that things in Gia's life were certainly not okay, and she started to finally believe she needed help. She knew she couldn't teach, and she started to feel some serious guilt and shame about being in charge of nine-year-olds while her life was such a disaster. Financially, she says she was totally "screwed" because she was spending so much money on laxatives. Today, Gia is still paying off the debt. She started out owing $16,000 and is now down to $6,000. She closed up her apartment and moved closer to her parents in order to seek treatment.

But she still wasn't quite ready to commit. She was home, and her mom had the idea that if she were around her family, it would all go away. The years of drinking, bingeing, and purging would just disappear. Of course they didn't, and Gia drank more, binged more, and purged more. Her mom had always stayed in the background, but she came home one day and found Gia passed out in her dad's favorite leather chair. That might not have been so bad if Gia hadn't urinated in the chair. Her mother finally took a stand and said, "You are a disaster. You are a mess, Gia!" And Gia left.

She lived in her car for a couple of weeks. She drank and parked, drank and parked. She finally got so sick of it she went to her parents' house at about 4 a.m. to apologize. They told her they had been so worried they had the police looking for her and the church praying for her. Gia is not sure about all this because she was right down the road

"Where do you go but home?"

in a parking lot and could have been found easily. They thought she was out at bars, but Gia was an isolator. She hid. Her dad was not sympathetic. Gia believes that has a lot to do with his own addictions. He didn't want to hear anything she had to say and instead told her to forget where they lived and don't come home.

Where do you go but home? Gia had no apartment, no job, and no friends. Friends? Not one. No one could be let in on her secrets. All she knew is that she needed to go somewhere. That somewhere was a treatment center. She just showed up, and when they told her she needed to go to detox first, all she could say was "No! I need to stay here." They did not make her go to detox. She entered a ninety-day program and stayed for six months. Gia was in love with it and didn't want to leave. Gia was still in her early twenties and describes this treatment center as a "bottom-barrel kind of place." It was primarily for prostitutes, jailed women, homeless women, and women from the reservation. Gia loved it because there were no egos.

She talked to her dad on occasion but refused to speak to her mom. She wanted no relationship with her at all because she was angry. It wasn't that Gia was angry over the chair incident but that she had refused to see that Gia had needed her help all those years. Six months later, though, the relationship with both parents had healed. Maybe it healed because Gia had to be strong for her little sister who had been diagnosed with a borderline personality disorder and had recently hit her bottom.

Gia's sister was said to have abandonment issues. Gia believes she has them also based on emotional abandonment. For the first fifteen years of her life, her dad was drunk or high. Because of this behavior as well as his womanizing, Gia's mom was depressed and unsatisfied with her own life. She threatened to leave her husband all the time but never did. Gia believes her mom had checked out. If she or her sister was upset, her mom would have no response. She showed no emotional engagement. Perhaps, Gia says, it was just the way her parents raised her, but she and her sister "used every substance we could get our hands on to feel—or to not feel."

After leaving rehab, Gia moved to a different city with a boyfriend she had known for many years. He was a carbon copy of her dad. It was difficult for Gia to stay sober, but she was working a 12-Step recovery program, attending meetings, and had a sponsor. Still, she did not have the everyday support from her boyfriend that she desperately needed. Gia decided to apply for a position as a flight attendant and was quickly engaged. She received her six-month sobriety chip while she was in training.

Wouldn't it be great if that were the end and there was not one more drink or bottom left?

It certainly would. But the truth of the matter is that Gia would say her story hadn't even begun yet!

While Gia was now working full-time as a flight attendant, she was honestly not in a very safe place. She relapsed any number of times. No one who knew her was around to make her feel bad about drinking. When you fly, you end up in an unfamiliar city with a hotel room to yourself for three days. Secrets galore, according to Gia. She went back to drinking on weeklong binges.

All the while she was binge drinking, she was also falling in love. She and her new boyfriend bought a house together; he asked her to marry him, and she was thrilled. Whether or not she continued to drink was not as important to her as the fact that she would have some sort of stability in her life. But that was not to be. Before a wedding date could be set, the love of her life told her there was no way he was going to get married. Gia says she did not see it coming, and she was ready to "sign out." She figured that as of that time, everyone in her life knew she was an alcoholic, so what the hell? Her love had just left her, so who could blame her?

She even asked her dad, "What would you do?" He said, "Drink." And so she did. Gia says she was saying good-bye. She had planned for a friend to take care of her animals; her sister could have all her stuff. She was ready to go. The problem was she was drinking and drinking and couldn't seem to get drunk enough to be numb. It wasn't working. Her friends kept telling her she had to get help, but she insisted that wasn't going to happen. Fortunately, her friends did not give up on her. They got her out of bed and put her into detox. It was Mother's Day, and even her mom, who never recognized Gia's addictions, asked her to do this. Gia called work and was ready to lose her job. "Fire me! I don't care." Her man had left her, and nothing else mattered after that.

After Gia left detox and went home, she found about six or seven cards from leaders of her company. They were handwritten, she tells me, and each asked, "What can we do?" and assured her to "Take all the time you need." Gia was astounded! They wanted to help? They didn't want to fire her? Even after those "miracles," as Gia calls them, she still didn't want to be sober. She was still alone and still sad.

She no longer wanted to die and decided that the least she could do was to get to a 12-Step meeting. After the meeting, as she was walking to her car, one of the members whom Gia describes as an "older Native American guy" stopped her. Gia had seen him numerous times at meetings in the past, and she always thought he was sleeping. He never said a word. So she was a bit taken aback when he approached her. He asked her if she had ever heard of a sweat lodge. She had not. He told her he was setting one up at the reservation, and he thought she would really enjoy it. She was so desperate to not feel the sadness within her she wasn't even thinking when she accepted the invitation. All she said was, "I'll be there." She had no idea what to expect.

Gia took a friend with her. She found out that the sleepy guy was an elder of the tribe, and he told her everything about the tradition, the symbols, and what was going to happen. He went through a very lengthy explanation. He said, "Everything you sweat out in there during the four rounds of intensive heat you can choose to leave there." Gia says that his *The sweat lodge was her rehab, and the elder her interventionist.* description was so beautiful you couldn't possibly make it up, not in your wildest imagination!

They went into the sweat lodge. Gia sat through the entire ceremony and sobbed and sobbed. She prayed for the elders to take away the sadness. She wanted it so bad, and she had been told that if you are desperate enough and willing, you will get this out of every cell of your body. The elder warned her that some people leave the sweat lodge and want to pick their issues back up because it is comfortable. Gia left hers there. She came out a different person. Gia says that she walked out of the sweat lodge in the middle of the desert and saw a blanket of stars. She looked at her friend and said, "I can't believe the experience. I just can't believe it." Gia says she has not wanted a drink since. She can talk about her boyfriend leaving and be okay with it. The sweat lodge was her rehab, and the elder her interventionist.

Gia is still amazed at how it all happened. She is still trying to grasp how this man who never spoke a word reached out to her. He hadn't asked anyone else to the sweat lodge. When she asked him why he chose her, he said he could see her desperation, sadness, and willingness. Gia says that the universe shifted for her that night, and it was never the same again. For the first time in her life, Gia has not wanted a drink. It is not even a thought. She still works on her eating disorders, although any episodes of purging are very few and far between.

The people Gia has met at the sweat lodge have found sobriety there. Today Gia believes that there are many different aspects to recovery, and it is her choice to use the sweat lodge. Gia still believes that a 12-Step program is important but that recovery doesn't have to be one-sided.

Gia is sober and happier than she has probably ever been in her life. She is in her early thirties today. She has lived a hundred lifetimes through her experiences but because of persevering has an incredibly happy, fulfilling future.

Resources

YOU CAN FIND ANYTHING YOU need by typing it in the browser of your computer. Here are a few of the sites that I recommend, and from these as a base you'll find other links that might be of interest. Make sure you check to see if you have an employee-assistance program (EAP) in the workplace. These can provide a tremendous amount of help and are confidential.

Adult Children of Alcoholics (ACOA)	*www.adultchildren.org*
Alcoholics Anonymous (AA)	*www.aa.org*
AA Online Intergroup	*www.aa-intergroup.org*
Al-Anon & Al-Ateen	*www.alanon-alateen.org*
Al-Anon Online Outreach	*www.ola-is.org*
Algamus Recovery Centers (gambling)	*www.algamus.org*
Association of Intervention Specialists (AIS)	*http://associationof interventionspecialists.org*
Cocaine Anonymous	*www.ca.org*

Compulsive Eaters Anonymous	www.ceahow.org
Co-Dependents Anonymous	www.coda.org
Crystal Meth Anonymous	www.crystalmeth.org
Eating Disorders Anonymous (EDA)	www.eatingdisorders anonymous.org
Families Anonymous	www.familiesanonymous .org
Gamblers Anonymous	www.gamblersanonymous .org
Gam-Anon (family/ friends of gamblers)	www.gam-anon.org
Love Addicts Anonymous	www.loveaddicts.org
Marijuana Anonymous	www.marijuana-anonymous.org
Narcotics Anonymous	www.na.org
National Council on Alcoholism and Drug Dependence	www.ncadd.org
Nicotine Anonymous	www.nicotine-anonymous .org
NotMYKid	www.notmykid.org
Overeaters Anonymous	www.oa.org
QuitNet (nicotine)	www.quitnet.com
Sex Addicts Anonymous	www.sexaa.org
Sex Love Addicts Anonymous	www.slaafws.org
Sonoran Healing Center (sex addiction)	www.sexual-addiction-recovery.com

Professional counselors and interventionists have credentials. Here is a list of some of the credentials and what they signify:

ACA	American Counseling Association
BRI-I	Board Certified Interventionist (drugs/alcohol)
BRI-II	Board Certified Interventionist (all addictions)
CCAS	Certified Clinical Addiction Specialist
CCGC	Certified Compulsive Gambling Counselor
CRC	Certified Recovery Coach
CSAT	Certified Sex Addiction Therapist
DBH	Doctor of Behavioral Health
LCSW	Licensed Social Worker
LISAC	Licensed Independent Substance Abuse Counselor
LMFT	Licensed Marriage Family Therapist
LPC	Licensed Professional Counselor
NCGC	Nationally Certified Gambling Counselor

You can read all my articles about addiction and 12-Step Recovery at *www.bellaonline.com/site/12steprecovery.* You can also write to me at *gratefulrecovery@gmail.com.*

About the Author

Kathy L. has been the 12-step recovery editor for BellaOnline since 2007, writing weekly articles on a variety of topics to support readers throughout their addiction recovery. Her articles have been used to help counselors, therapists, support groups, and individuals. She holds a degree in education with an emphasis on counseling. She is a mother and grandmother and currently resides in Arizona.

To Our Readers

CONARI PRESS, AN IMPRINT OF Red Wheel/Weiser, publishes books on topics ranging from spirituality, personal growth, and relationships to women's issues, parenting, and social issues. Our mission is to publish quality books that will make a difference in people's lives—how we feel about ourselves and how we relate to one another. We value integrity, compassion, and receptivity, both in the books we publish and in the way we do business.

Our readers are our most important resource, and we appreciate your input, suggestions, and ideas about what you would like to see published.

Visit our website *www.redwheelweiser.com* where you can subscribe to our newsletters and learn about our upcoming books, exclusive offers, and free downloads.

You can also contact us at *info@redwheelweiser.com*.

Conari Press
an imprint of Red Wheel/Weiser, LLC
665 Third Street, Suite 400
San Francisco, CA 94107

N Webster Comm Public Library
301 N Main St. PO Box 825
North Webster, IN 46555